About the author

Sterling is an independent, fee-only financial planner at Blankenship Financial Planning in New Berlin, IL. He earned a PhD in financial and retirement planning from the American College of Financial Services. He is also a Senior Lecturer of Finance at the University of Illinois at Urbana-Champaign. He contributes to the blog *Getting Your Financial Ducks in A Row*, where he writes regularly about investments, retirement savings, and financial planning.

Sterling's writing has appeared in MarketWatch, Forbes, AdviceIQ, Business Insider, USA Today, NAPFA Planning Perspectives, and The Motley Fool among others.

Sterling lives in Springfield, IL with his daughters. In his spare time, he enjoys fly fishing, beekeeping, the outdoors, chickens (yes, chickens), gardening, and time with his family.

Dedication

To my my daughters Madeline and Delaney — happiness is balance, and you are my counterweights. I love you.

Acknowledgements

I want to acknowledge the efforts of my friends and colleagues who graciously invested their time and energy in the genesis of this book:

Jessea Negless (cover design), Jason Raskie, Dan Pink, Geoff Briggs, Trevor Raskie, Jane Gibbons, Karl Samson, Dan & Jody Lack, Todd Marquardt, Bryan Strike, Leah Wilson, and my parents, John and Sharon.

Your time and wisdom is invaluable – I am forever grateful.

A special thank you goes to Jim Blankenship for his input, edits and suggestions on making this book readable and generally more tolerable for the reader. *Thanks Jim!* I said.

Introduction

This book is a beginning, a place to start and a reference to come to when the need arises. More importantly it is meant to be *moved on* from as you explore more fitness and financial concepts to better improve your life and overall happiness.

This book is not a cure all nor is it meant to provide the end all be all for your fitness and financial woes or concerns. I highly recommend you seek additional help, advice and professional opinions from qualified, competent professionals as you continue to learn and grow – personally and professionally.

It goes without saying that before you start any fitness program – consult with your doctor or physician. The same is true regarding a financial plan – utilize the resources and knowledge of a professional financial planner. Your due diligence is a must.

Finally, should you have questions, please feel free to contact me at sterling.raskie@gmail.com.

Good luck!

LOSE WEIGHT, SAVE MONEY

Eat right and exercise.

Yeah right.

We've all heard that before. Numerous times throughout the day we are drilled by those famous last words, hearing them either on TV, the radio, heck, even from our own loved ones. But has anyone ever told us what exactly that means?

What is "eating right?" Low-carb? No-carb? High protein? No fast food? Drink your weight in water every day? Drink celery juice? If your head isn't spinning yet, you're one of the lucky ones. That famous saying seems to be everyone's fallback, their cushion, and their catchphrase - yet no one really has an actual answer.

$500 bucks later, there you sit, with another useless piece of ab equipment and a half-eaten "protein" bar that tastes like God-knows-what, but certainly not like the "velvety chocolate" flavor advertised on the case of them you bought last week.

So you decide to give it another day or two, and that lasts about 5 minutes into your next workout when you throw in the towel, **again**, and go back to the one thing that never scolded you to eat right and exercise, never called you fat, but always welcomed you with open arms: your refrigerator. And you continue on a downward spiral until you decide to try again, and again, and again...

To tell you the truth, this program isn't the answer either.

"What?" you might be asking. Well, it isn't. It's merely a guide to help you along your journey, a journey that will last the rest of your life.

Much like yourself, I, too, thought that there had to be some magic formula, some secret potion that would drop the weight right off and in two days I would be ready to show the world the new me. Not so.

The answer is you. Yes, you. You are the only person that can change your thoughts, your habits, and your self-image. I can't do it, and neither can anyone or anything else, no matter what they promise. It all starts with making a conscious decision that you are ready to change – for the better. And it starts within you. It starts by changing your thought processes and how you see yourself from the inside out. As the saying goes, **"Wherever the head goes, the body follows."**

The same is true for your mind. **Wherever your mind goes, your body follows**.

As I said before, this program is not a cure-all, nor is it the only way to reach your personal fitness and financial goals. I don't claim to be an expert on fitness and finances. What I do claim is that if you follow your goals, learn to think differently, and take it one day at a time – heck, one hour at a time – you'll be well on your way to the new and exciting life that awaits you.

Before you read any further, think about what challenges you have faced before. How did they affect you? How did they affect others? Did you learn from them? Did you give up? Did you overcome those challenges?

Think about your answers. Are you ready to make a change in your life? Or are you just going to put this aside like all the other programs and gadgets you've tried, now broken and defeated?

I'm going to be brutally honest with you: if you don't think you can do this, then you probably won't. If you've given up before you've even started, then send the program back and get your money so you can spend it on cookies and ice cream. I don't want you to have it. There's someone out there who needs this more than you. And I would rather refund your money and get this program back than have it collect dust when someone else will score a big win from it.

So, if you're really and truly in, then where in the heck do we begin?

The answer is here.

When? Now!

There is never a better time to start than now. We must get rid of those old saying such as

"I'll start tomorrow."

"After this weekend, I'm going to make a change."

"I swear that was the last time I eat like that for a long time."

Don't worry; I've been guilty of this, too. It happens to a lot of people. The biggest change you can make in your life is to act now. Because we both know that **"someday" never comes**.

As Henry Ford said, "If you think you can, you will. If you think you can't, you won't. Either way, you're right."

If you're serious about your success, then you've made the first step toward becoming a different you. Congratulations! One of the hardest parts is over. And as you know: **wherever the mind goes, the body follows.**

You can do it.

ONE DAY AT A TIME

You are a unique individual compared to others. The only difference lies in everyone's ability to see not who they are now, but who they want to become – and making the decision to think and act in that way. In the fitness portion of this program, we will go over how to write and study goals.

Like the goals-setting skills you will develop, for which you tell yourself in the present tense that you have already become something or already achieved something, **you need to act with confidence and positivity on a day-to-day basis**. Act as if you've already lost the weight. Act as if your bank account is already full of money. When you think and act in this way, you're automatically programming your mind to think it's already happened. It has no choice but to fulfill your destiny. **Where the mind goes, the body follows**.

The most important thing I want you to remember from here on in is that we're going to do this **one day at a time.** As the saying goes,

"Rome wasn't built in a day." Great masterpieces, chiseled sculptures, vintage wines – all take time to reach their true potential, their finished perfection. You need to realize that this change in your habits and in your life will not happen overnight. There are going to be times when you are frustrated. There are going to be days when you do your workouts haphazardly. This happens to everyone.

There have been days when all I wanted to do was sleep in, sit on the couch all day, and eat nothing but pizza and ice cream. And there are days I have done that. I could lie to you and say that there hasn't been a single time where I've gone off track, never missed a workout, and always ate what I knew I was supposed to.

That just isn't the case.

There are days when I cheat. There are going to be days when you will give in to temptation as well. Here's the key: remember that **each day is a new day**. If you fall off track, get back on. Believe me, it's that easy. The last thing you want to do is give up on yourself because of small setbacks. Just stick to your plan, review your goals, and keep moving forward.

Think about it this way: if you set a goal to lose 1 pound per week — a very attainable goal indeed — you'll have lost over 50 pounds in one year! Takes it **one day at a time**.

With your money and finances, it's going to be the same way.

HOW DO I SAVE MONEY?

This may sound like an easy question to some, for others it's a most mysterious concept, one that has eluded them for most of their lives. Where do I start? With what money can I even do this? Below, you'll find a few examples of how you can turn bad eating habits into money in the bank. It's going to take some self-discipline at first, but after a while, it will become a habit – a good one!

Some of you have a habit of going to the local coffee shop or bakery every morning for that latte, cappuccino, or scone that you don't even think twice of when you're buying it. But have you ever taken time to consider what's in that latte or scone that's going into your body when you eat it? If you haven't guessed by now, the answer is a lot of sugar and refined, processed, simple carbohydrates. This has a very negative impact on your body, not to mention the start of your day.

Simple carbohydrates like those found in the table sugar, and the bleached flour that go into making the scone, donut, or croissant, have a very negative effect on your metabolism. Simple carbohydrates like these force your body to digest them very quickly, causing a rapid spike in your insulin levels. This means that as insulin levels increase, your body's ability and desire to make fat is very high. What you normally experience is a "sugar rush," in which you have a lot of energy at first, then, an hour or so later, you crash, feeling tired, sleepy, or even crabby. This does not help the rest of your day go smoothly.

Then, of course, you feel hungry again, and grab a "healthy" snack of pretzels, popcorn, or whatever else is in the vending machine, and the downward spiral continues. Or you might wait to eat until lunch or even the end of the day when you're absolutely starving, and as soon as you get home, you tear into the sweetest, tastiest thing you can get your hands on.

AVOID THE TRAP

It can be tempting to get coffee every day, go out to lunch, or hit the vending machine whenever the urge arises. Coffee easily goes for $2-$3 at a coffee shop – sometimes even more. Then there's the additional pastry, scone, etc. to complement the coffee. Instead, why not make your coffee at home? Invest in a coffee maker and thermos if you need more coffee later.

Next, pocket the $2-$3 that you would have spent on the latte and scone. Put it in a jar, put it in the bank, put it anywhere you can save it. There's a great start! Think about it. $2-$3 per day times an average of 30 days is an extra $60-$90 in your pocket every month!

Now, if you eat fast food at lunch or find yourself eating out a lot, make a commitment to pack your lunch. Resist the temptation to go to lunch with your office all the time. If you go to lunch daily, that will average $5-$10 per lunch, at least. That's an extra $100-$200 saved! Put them together and you've saved $160-$290 – in one month!

I'm not saying never go out to lunch. I have friends of mine that I meet for lunch every now and again. The point being that I don't make a habit of it. On the other hand, once **you** have made a habit of saving this extra money and have learned to discipline yourself to save, then it's not going to hurt you to go out occasionally.

Does It Really Cost More to Eat Healthy?*

From time to time I will hear the argument that it's expensive to eat healthy to lose weight or maintain a healthy lifestyle. What I want to do is provide some information based on my own experience that may help give a counter argument to this belief.

While I am not disagreeing entirely that eating healthily is more expensive than not, I am saying that if done carefully, it is possible to eat healthily for less than what it would cost for less heathy alternatives.

One of the arguments I hear is that individuals may be overweight due to relying on fast food menu items – especially those on dollar or value menus. And the reason these menus are relied on is because shopping for a healthy alternative is pricier.

Let's take a look.

Consider a few value menu items from a well-known fast-food provider.

Cheeseburger - $1 – 300 calories.
Small fries - $1 – 230 calories.
Small soft drink - $1 – 150 calories.

Total cost for the meal is $3. Total calories are 680.

This may be a bit extreme, but I am going to calculate this for three meals per day, for 7 days a week. This totals to $9 per day, or $63 for the week. Total calories are 2,040 for the day, or 14,280 for the week. Remember, this is off the dollar menu. Dine-in restaurants are likely much pricier.

In comparison, the local grocery store sells whole grain tortilla wraps for $4.96 a package, containing 16 wraps. This amounts to $0.31 per wrap.

One dozen eggs is about $1.99 or roughly $0.17 per egg (full disclosure: I have my own chickens, so I don't pay for my eggs).

Simply cook two eggs, season with salt and pepper and put in the wrap. Voila!

Assuming this meal was eaten every meal, every day for a week (boring and dull, but doable) this amounts to:

Wrap - $0.31 – 100 calories.
2 eggs - $0.34 – 160 calories.
Glass of water - Free – 0 calories.

The total for each meal is $0.65, or $1.95 daily. This is $13.65 weekly. Total daily calories are 780, which is 5,460 weekly.

Some readers may need to eat more, so doubling this (six small meals per day) would be 1,560 daily and 10,920 weekly calories respectively. If more is needed, simply have two wraps and four eggs (my usual breakfast).

At three meals per day, this is a weekly savings of just over $49. At six meals, it's just over $35 saved.

Am I arguing that one should live just on wraps and eggs alone? No. The point is that with some planning and education, it can be possible to eat healthy, for less than what an unhealthy alternative would be.

Substitutions can be made for the wrap such as whole grain bread ($1.75 a loaf), lettuce ($1.99 for a pound bag) and other substitutes for the egg such as chicken, beef, venison, etc.

Don't be afraid to experiment on your own and see what you can come up with!

*Note: This excerpt comes from my book *Coffee Table Personal Finance: An Easy to Follow Personal Finance Guide*

PAY YOURSELF FIRST

Now that you're saving money, you're going to get yourself on an automatic pay plan. You're going to learn to **pay yourself first**. Even if it's only a minimal amount, that doesn't matter. What does matter is that you are going to **pay yourself first**. This concept is found in the book, *The Richest Man in Babylon* by George S. Clason. Consider yourself the first bill you must pay.

Here's how you can apply this to your life:

First, one of the easiest things you can do is take a portion of your paycheck and stick it right in the bank, right away, the day you get paid. One of the best ways I know of to accomplish this is through the genius of direct deposit. If your employer allows it, have your paycheck directly deposited into your bank account every payday. Some employers even allow a net direct deposit and a fixed direct deposit.

Net direct deposit involves most of your paycheck going into your checking or savings account.

Fixed direct deposit entails a small portion of the same paycheck going into a different account. You can make this any amount you wish, but for now, I recommend you start small. You can always add more at another time.

The beauty of this system is that you ***automatically*** put money into a separate savings account, and you never have to worry about spending it, cashing a paycheck and physically putting the money into the account, or trying to remember to save the money in the first place. After a few months, you may even forget about it until you receive your bank statement and see a nice sum of money already growing!

And you're still living comfortably on what's left!

Another thing you can do – if you get paid by paper check – is to set up a savings account with an automatic bill payment service. That way, when you cash your check and deposit it into your account, each month on a specific date a certain sum of money will be withdrawn from your checking account, into your savings account to pay the bills. This is the same as paying your bills online, or having your bills automatically taken out of your account. Treat your new savings account like you would a bill – never miss a payment.

Never.

I recommend starting out by saving 15-25% of your income. If that's a stretch for you, start saving 10%, 5%, or even 1%. The main point is to start – now! You'll be amazed at how quickly it grows, and how easy it becomes to save even more. A funny thing happens when your money grows: it attracts more money. You'll become motivated to save greater and greater amounts. You'll be excited when you look at your account and it may even put you in a good mood.

Of course, money doesn't buy happiness, but can you remember how you felt the last time you found a $5-dollar bill or a $10-dollar bill? Heck, even a buck! Felt pretty good, didn't it?

10% CAN ADD UP

We just talked about paying yourself first, right?

Now let's see what happen when you do that, and even better, what happens when you give yourself a raise (Yes, you *can* do that!). Let's say you start saving a reasonable amount of $100 per month. If you did that every month for 30 years at a conservative rate of 5% compounded annually, you'd have a tidy sum of $83,577. Not bad, right? Now, let's say you decide to give yourself a one-time raise after a year – a raise of 10%. Now you're saving $110 per month for the remaining 29 years. Your tidy sum has now grown to $95,508 – for only a paltry $10 extra per month!

Now, let's pretend you decide to give yourself an annual raise of 10% each year for 30 years. And ask yourself, "Who can't afford 10% more?" Think of it this way – you're taking baby steps. $10 extra per month in year 2, $11 extra per month in year 3 and so on. By the time you've reached year 30, you'll have saved $169,105. All by simply taking baby steps. All for just an additional

10% annually (insert overly excited infomercial guru here)!

The main idea is the get in the habit of not only saving but giving yourself a raise and increasing the amount you save periodically. You don't want to fall into the trap of saving $50 per month, then forgetting about it. Granted, you'll at least have something after 30 years ($41,613 for those of you keeping track) but we both know that costs of living increase, inflation rears its ugly head, daddy needs a new pair of shoes…you get it.

HOW INTEREST IS FIGURED

Comparing interest rates for certificates of deposit? You will see the terms APY (Annual Percentage Yield) and APR (Annual Percentage Rate) in the brochure. What does each mean and how are they different?

APR is the account's headline number. For example, if you invest $1,000 in a one-year CD that pays 5%, that means the CD's APR is 5%. So it seems as if the account makes 5% ($50) for the year for a total of $1,050. But this might not actually be the case.

APY considers how often that interest rate is credited. Does it credit a portion of that 5% monthly, semi-annually or annually? If it's annually, you still get the 5% or $50.

If it's semi-annually, you get credited 2.5% every six months. This is a bit better since you can reinvest that interest payment ($25) for the remaining six months on the CD. Now, compound interest takes effect and your balance is at $1,025 after six months. That $1,025 now gets to partake in the remaining 2.5% that evolves over the next 6 months. This adds up to slightly more than the $1,050 balance that annual compounding brings you. Being credited or compounded semi-annually leaves you with $1,050.63 at the end of one year.

If that $1,000 is credited (compounded) monthly you're at $1,051.16 when it matures. As you can see, the more compounding periods you have, the better. This is the miracle of compound interest and the time value of money.

On the other hand, compounding interest works against us when we borrow money. Before you take out a home or auto loan or credit card, note how often the interest rate is calculated as well as the APR rate.

Generally, certificates of deposit are very safe, 100% guaranteed by the Federal Deposit Insurance Corp. They do give you some yield, but unlike the example above, they aren't known for generosity.

As of this writing, the best offer for a one-year CD is 1.05% APY with a minimum investment of

$5,000. At this rate, you do not even keep with inflation. In fact, you lose money. The latest government inflation figures show that consumer prices rose 1.7% over the course of 2012. And this is below average. Average inflation has historically been 3-4%.

Of course, if you don't need the funds any time soon (most CDs charge high fees for early withdrawal), putting your money into a CD is better than letting it sit in your checking account to be slowly eroded by inflation.

Look into CD and savings offers from online banks. As long as they are FDIC-insured, you have nothing to worry about. Without the expense of brick-and-mortar banks, online banks usually offer a better yield.

THE LAW OF RECIPROCITY

As your wealth accumulates and continues to grow, there is a law I want you to be mindful of and respect. You don't have to follow it, but believe me, it will pay you more than any bank, investment, mutual fund, or stock could ever do. I'm talking about **the law of reciprocity**. Some call it tithing, luck, karma, reaping what you sow, give and take. Whatever you want to call it, it works. And I highly recommend that you do it.

Following the law of reciprocity means giving a little of what you make. It could mean giving to your favorite charity, your church, a friend in need, a homeless shelter, or any other cause or helpful service in your community. **The point is to give**. And it will come back to you in droves. Don't ask me how it works, it just does. I promise you that. Consider this for a moment: money is called currency for a reason. Like any current, it was meant to flow, to travel, to move. And the more you give, the more comes back to you. I promise.

WHAT TO DO WITH YOUR MONEY

After a while, you're going to have a sizeable amount of money in your savings account. There are a few choices you can make on where to put your money to work. You can leave it in your savings account. You can invest in stocks, bonds, and real estate, or you can even start a side business. What I recommend you do first, if you're going to invest, is take the time to invest in your financial education. You work hard for your money. Don't lose it all to ignorance. You want your money to work hard for you, and in this case, as in so many others, **knowledge is power**.

There are several excellent books (other than the one you hold in your hand) that can provide some outstanding knowledge of money, how it works, and some of the best practices for your money. Each person is different so I would recommend exploring and reading a few to see which you like and works best for you.

Ultimately, it's your money. What you do with it is your business. If you decide not to do anything, at least keep it in your savings account. And keep it there until you know what your next step will be. There, it's at least guaranteed up to $250,000 by the FDIC. Investing without knowing what you're investing in or without knowing what the investment is about is very risky – and it can be a recipe for disaster. You may also consider working with a competent professional, such as a CERTIFIED FINANCIAL PLANNER™, or another qualified professional. I would recommend consulting with a fee-only planner or firm. Fee-only planners are paid on their advice, not from selling a product. In addition, they are also required to be *fiduciaries*. This means that they are *legally required* to act in your best interest – not theirs. It's a quick way to narrow down a few planners and advisors to interview so that you can find one that fits you and your needs.

A MONEY BACK GUARANTEE

You've heard the saying before that there are a few guarantees in life: death and taxes. I'd also like to add another: guaranteeing yourself a rate of return. I get asked this question frequently, usually by someone who's a conservative investor or someone looking for a "sure thing".

This is what I tell them, and I am telling you. Call this your money back guarantee.

For the majority of readers, this will come into play as most of you have debt in some form or another. Whether it's your mortgage, automobile, boat, credit cards, college, many Americans have different amounts of debt all at different interest rates. Typically, your consumer debt (credit cards) is going to have the highest interest rates.

Here's how to guarantee yourself a rate of return: PAY DOWN YOUR DEBT. By paying down your debt you will be guaranteeing yourself the rate of return equal to the interest rate you're paying on the debt. For example, let's say you have credit card debt of 15% on a balance of

$10,000. Want to guarantee yourself a rate of return of 15%? Pay off your credit card. And fast. Do me a favor. Go on the Internet and search for a minimum payment calculator for credit cards. Many cards are now showing this in the fine print on their statements. For my example, I put in $10,000 debt at 15% interest and a minimum payment of $200. After 30 years, yes 30 *years*, the total payments made on that $10,000 of debt are $25,573 – and I still owe! An easy way to look at this is let's say you paid off the card right away with $10,000. Right off the bat, you'll have saved over $15,000 by *not* making minimum payments. If you're starting anew and this whole paying off debt thing is alien to you, try upping your payments (baby steps) or even getting rid of "luxury" items you don't *need* until your debt is paid off, like cable TV, dining out, etc. and put that monthly cable TV, dining out money, etc., toward the debt you owe.

My suggestion would be to start on the highest interest rate debt you have first and then pay down from there. Once you've paid down that debt, move to the next highest interest rate and so on. Some people are in favor of starting on the smallest amount of debt first and going from there. The reasoning being that you can build momentum by getting at least something paid off quickly. From a strictly monetary standpoint, you'll save more money paying down higher debt first, but feel free to use whichever method you prefer. Just do something!

Another idea when you start paying down your debt is to tack on an additional 10% *or more* on what you're currently paying and keep increasing that percentage monthly or annually until you can pay it off in full. It's the same as the 10% toward saving more money, just used to pay down debt quicker.

One debt that you can consider just paying the regular monthly payments on is your mortgage. Nothing wrong with paying it down early – do it if you can. Given today's interest rates being low, it's not as big of a deal as 15% in credit card interest rates is. Plus, you can deduct the interest on your mortgage. In addition, with mortgage rates low, a better investment return may be achieved elsewhere in the market, however, that extra return is not guaranteed. That being said, over 15 years or 30 years as most mortgages are, there's a high likelihood of better returns.

One final caveat to consider is this: once you've paid off a debt, act as though you still have to make the payment only this time (you guess it) pay yourself first. Continue to pay that "bill" only now direct it to your savings, IRA, college fund, etc.

KEEPING UP WITH THE JONESES

In grade school we call it "trying to make friends". In high school we called it "peer pressure". In adulthood we call it "keeping up the Joneses". The keeping up with the Joneses mentality has a considerable effect on many, if not all of us. We just have differences in what we're trying to keep up with – mostly material things such as cars, SUVs, colleges, homes, clothing, etc. Much of this peer pressure is indirect – meaning that our peers and friends rarely come out and pressure us into buying certain things or spending certain amounts, but rather it's us seeing what they have, and thinking we need the same thing, the same dream and the same lifestyle. This is what gets many people into trouble.

Take for example the recent college graduate. Having spent the last 4 to 6 years living off Ramen noodles and corn flakes, they suddenly find themselves in a position of extreme income influx, but with little to none financial literacy. Instinctively, they feel a need to reward themselves for many years of hard work, and often see friends that have graduated just before them or in similar careers, suddenly driving the new sedan, living in the nice house and enjoying the American Dream. After all, why work so hard in college if not to get a well-paying job to afford all those things they really *need*. Suddenly, it's 10 years later and they're over-leveraged (taking on too much debt), they're 5 figures or more in credit card debt, and they find themselves wishing they were back in college. Ramen looks a whole lot better at this point!

Seasoned adults are no different. We experience the same mentality and the same temptations. It's no different than when we were kids. We still want toys; it's just that the toys are much more expensive now. We see a neighbor drive home in a new SUV, our close friends just bought their dream home, the Joneses are sending their kids to Ivy League schools – living the high life. Again, this indirect peer pressure can ruin our financial plans and our hopes for a secure retirement.

And it can be easy to fall prey to the temptation.

For example, would I like a new car? Certainly (I drive a 2002 minivan with over 312,000 miles) – there are times when I am driving down the road and I see a nice sedan or SUV go by and I think, "Wow – that'd be nice to have." Here's something that has helped me and may be beneficial for you is to have a mental checklist to run through – something that will help calm you down and have a clear mind about what you should do next.

- Ask yourself, "Is this something I truly *need?*"
- Is it something that will improve my life, long-term?
- Can I wait?
- Can I *afford* it?
- Will this increase my net worth, or will it increase my debt?
- How happy will this make me?
- *Why* do I need this?

Now – am I saying you shouldn't have nice things or work to improve your life and better yourself? Not at all. What I am recommending (myself included) is that we look at what we really need, what really makes us happy, and forget what the Joneses are doing. Chances are – they're much *worse* off than we are.

41

FINANCIAL AUTONOMY

Recently, I had the opportunity to sit across from a couple nearing retirement, and looking for some options with regards to their cash flow needs, possible retirement dates, and the ever-present question, "Do we have enough?" Typically, these conversations involve careful consideration given to several different worries, fears and "big" problems that clients face. Frequently I will work with couples who have a hard time agreeing on how much they can spend in retirement, how much they can afford to save, and where to prioritize and allocate the money (to retirement, a wedding, college, etc.).

This couple, however, was different.

Well in position to enter retirement comfortable with little, if any to worry about, the tension between these two spouses could be cut with a knife – it was almost tough to sit through. One would snip at the other, and the other would interrupt while the snipping was happening to snip back. Small jabs, really – and nothing to get too excited about – at least in this practitioner's opinion. Were they arguing about needing more, where to save, who will work more? Not at all. They were arguing about the little things. One spouse was upset because the other spouse was spending money on a local community newspaper subscription, while the other was upset about spending on something similar.

After about 20 minutes of quasi-hostile bantering back and forth, they asked my opinion. And here's what I told them:

Autonomy.

I suggested that they each allocate a certain portion of their earnings each month to separate and personal checking accounts. I also suggested that other than knowing the amounts going in each month to each account, they needn't discuss the purchases they make from their respective, separate accounts – it was their money to do with what they wanted, from newspaper subscriptions to purchasing items for a hobby. The looks on their faces were of genuine consideration of the idea. And they seemed to relax just a bit in their chairs. This couple was brilliant on the big things but was letting the little things hamper their progress toward their financial planning goals. They left the office saying they would give it a try.

For couples I have recommended this to, the results have been extremely favorable. Many couples often report a sense of freedom, even though they may not feel chained down to their mutual budgets. Some have even reported using the money to buy gifts for the other spouse, relating back to the time when they were dating and such gifts were surprises, not expected and known purchases from the mutual account.

Financial autonomy can be a great tool in financial planning for couples. And sometimes being allowed to have some independent control on the little things, makes working together on the big things tolerable, if not enjoyable.

SIMPLE MATH

Your body can be a lot like your bank account in that, again, **knowledge is power**, and you need to know the right formulas for your efforts to equal success. Let me give you a little breakdown in terms of how your body uses the food you feed it. I hinted at this a bit earlier, but now I'm going to go into a little more detail.

For you to lose weight, you must consume less food than your body needs for fuel. Don't worry. This doesn't mean you are going to be starving yourself. Remember what that can do to you – slow your metabolism down – which is what we don't want.

There are about 3,500 calories in a pound. This means that to lose a pound of fat, we must take away 3,500 calories. This can be done easily if we do the math. By cutting out 500 calories per day, in seven days, that's one pound! And that's before we even started exercising!

Next, let's look at how your body reacts to certain foods. To begin, consider this: have you ever sat around a campfire? When you put dry wood or leaves on the fire what happens? They burn very quickly and very hot. But what happens when you put a soggy piece of wood on? It hisses and smokes and smolders. Sometimes it goes out. This is how your body treats refined sugars, white flour products, and junk food, in general.

For example, protein raises your body's metabolism by 30%, meaning that your inner fire burns hot. Carbohydrates – the soggy leaves of the food world – only raise it by 4%. The reason for this is that protein is harder for your body to digest. Therefore, your body must use more energy (burn more calories!) to digest it than it would carbohydrates.

Similar in effect is fiber and fibrous foods. Your body cannot digest fiber, which is why it's so good and cleansing for your body, particularly the digestive tract. It will still expend calories trying to digest the fiber, but to no avail. The good news is that you can eat a lot of fiber, and get and feel full, but not have to feel guilty, all while your body is burning calories trying to digest it. Some people refer to this as "negative calories," meaning that your body burns more energy than the food provides.

Fasting or Grazing?

Losing weight isn't as complicated as you may think. It's not as complicated as fad diets, media outlets, or the plethora of other misguided and bogus information you have seen. It is a simple as this:

Eat less, exercise more.

That's as complicated as it gets. This book covers how to do both. Here, we cover eating less. Eating less does not mean starving yourself. Far from it. It simply means in order to lose weight, you must burn more energy than you consume.

The extra energy your body needs will come from body fat. Over time, you'll notice that your body fat is decreasing. Since you're expending more calories through exercising than you're consuming through eating, your body will get the additional energy it needs from body fat. This is also true if you're *not* exercising.

What do I mean by that? I mean that you will still lose weight even if you don't exercise. The reason is that your body needs a certain amount of energy (calories) daily to exist – to survive. If it gets less energy than it needs, it will get the extra from stored body fat. If it gets more than it needs, it stores body fat. Exercising helps speed the process of using more calories (body fat) than you consume.

So how do we get started reducing calories. I'm going to provide two examples. I have done both and have gotten results with both methods. You will need to try and see which one works for you – or a combination of both.

Fasting

Fasting is the act of going without food for a certain period. This may mean skipping a meal (skipping breakfast is ideal – despite what you have heard that it's the most important meal of the day).

Fasting may also be only eating within a certain window during your day. For example, a person could fast 18 hours, and then eat only during a 6-hour window in the day. This is commonly known as intermittent fasting. Finally, fasting may be going an entire day (or longer) without food.

By default, fasting means you're consuming less food since you're not eating. Less food consumed means your body must get energy from somewhere. This will come from body fat, which in turn leads to weight loss. However, the temptation may be there to overeat when you break your fast. For this reason, I suggest you start fasting gradually, and don't go to extremes. The goal is to move forward, not backwards.

Start by skipping one meal (preferably breakfast) and go from there. Work your way to two meals and so on. One of the benefits of fasting is since you're eating fewer meals, you must consume more in the few meals you do eat to get the calories your body needs. For example, let's say your body needs 1,500 calories per day just to maintain itself and function properly. An 18-hour fast means you must get 1,500 calories in a 6-hour window. This means three meals of 500 calories each, two meals of 750 calories each or one meal if 1,500 calories.

Your body gets the calories it needs, yet you may feel fuller, more satiated due to consuming more calories in fewer meals.

When you fast, it means just that – you're not eating. Do not snack when you're fasting or think eating a protein bar or shake is part of your fast. Fasting means no eating. Period. The only things that can be consumed during a fast and it still be considered fasting are coffee (black), unsweetened tea, water, and seltzer water/club soda. Fasting or not, do not drink regular or diet sodas, juices, sweetened tea or coffee, sports drinks, etc.

Grazing

Grazing means you consume anywhere from four to six smaller meals throughout the day, spaced apart every two to four hours. I have found that grazing takes more planning, but it's doable.

Keeping with our above example of needing 1,500 calories per day, six small meals means 250 calories, five small meals means 300 calories, and four small meals means 375 calories per meal respectively.

The concept behind grazing is that you eat less food, but more frequently. You're still reducing calories, just using a different methodology. You may find this beneficial if you think it might be hard to fast initially, or if you don't trust yourself yet to fast and then break your fast without overconsuming – especially on junk food.

The type of eating method you choose will be determined by which one you feel works best for you. Personally, I have found that I prefer fasting over grazing. I have lost weight and kept in shape doing both. With fasting, I don't have to plan as much (less meals to plan, prepare, and pack) and it works for my schedule. My fasting schedule is generally fasting an entire day (usually Monday), once per week followed by intermittent fasting the remainder of the week with my cheat meal/day on Sunday. I also do a three-day fast every quarter.

However, you may find that grazing works better for you. This could be due to your work schedule, family/spouse work and eating schedules, and so on. When I grazed, I still fasted once per week.

It goes without saying that what you eat when fasting and reducing calories is critical. It makes no sense to fast for 18 hours just to spend 6 hours eating nothing but simple carbs, sugar, and junk food.

Soon, you'll notice that your body (and you) will be used to the change and reduction of food intake is no longer a drastic change. You'll also notice you'll have more energy, your clothes fit better, and you look better.

An indirect benefit of eating less whether through fasting or grazing will be the fact that you'll spend less money on food (since you're eating less, therefore buying less), and you'll be able to save that extra money. Determine exactly how much you're saving by tracking your spending (which you should already be doing). I have seen my grocery bill drop because of this. Soon you'll have done this long enough to determine a weekly or monthly grocery budget and you can plan accordingly.

A word of caution: *Never* grocery shop when you're hungry. You will be tempted to buy way more food than you need, and you'll likely buy food that you shouldn't be eating – like junk food. I suggest doing your grocery shopping after a meal or better yet, after a "cheat meal" or day. The reason for this is you will likely be so full and satiated that you'll only buy the groceries you know you need. There's less temptation to buy junk food, and there's less temptation to overspend since you're not hungry.

Food Autonomy (Cheat meal/day)

I used to weigh a good 265 pounds. That's about 75 pounds more than I weigh now. And I've been able to keep it off for about 20 years. How have I been able to do that? For me, it was easy at first. I was very motivated as the weight was coming off, and by the spring (I started my journey in January), I was down to less than 200 pounds. About a year later, after I had kept the weight off, I became stagnant and the temptation was much greater for me to cheat and not stick to my eating habits and goals. Why? Easy: I was struggling because during the first few months of my program, I never had that one day here and there when I allowed myself to eat whatever I wanted – a "cheat day" or "cheat meal". I never touched a piece of cake, candy, or sugar.

Granted the weight came off fast, but at the expense of me constantly craving sweets. Then I would binge. Not good. I would eat an entire package of cookies, or ice cream, whatever I could tear into. Then, I would get the post pig-out guilt, put on my running shoes and go running, feeling miserable.

I knew there had to be a better way. How could anyone forever banish themselves from junk food? Some folks can do it. I can't. That's when I started to read about giving myself one day per week to eat whatever I wanted. As I did more research, I found out that other fitness-minded people like me were doing the same thing. Some were doing it so that every three or four days they ate a "cheat meal", while others took one "cheat day" per week.

Personally, I like the one day per week model, using it has really helped me to stay on track, and I recommend you do the same. It's much easier to wait for six days and then have a day where you can eat whatever you want, than to deal with the mental games you'll play stressing out over whether you've sabotaged your weight loss goals by cheating during the week at one meal. You can call this, "food autonomy."

BE PREPARED

If you graze, there are going to be days when things don't go as planned. The kids are going to be sick, or have a game, or you must stay late at work, or the car breaks down, and on, and on. You need to be prepared by having some emergency food stored somewhere that you can use at times like these. For example, at some time or another I have kept a couple of protein bars in the glove compartment of my car. Other times, I have kept a shaker bottle, a bottle of water, and a package of protein on hand so that I can make a quick shake.

When you go to the health food store, ask them for MRPs (Meal Replacement Powders). These can take the place of a meal and come in handy when you need a quick bite. At my office, I always have a couple of cans of tuna, sardines, and even a shaker bottle with some protein. That way, if I forget to pack my lunch, I'm covered. The last thing you want to happen is to have something stressful occur, and not be able to eat for a long time. By the time the crisis is averted, you're starving, and looking for a little condolence. You open the fridge and forget all your goals for just a second... Be careful! This can be dangerous. **Always be prepared.**

HOLIDAYS AND SPECIAL OCCASIONS

Holidays and specials occasions such as birthdays, graduations, bah mitzvahs, weddings, can be a very tempting time to fall off track and lose sight of your end target – a healthier you. Don't panic. **Just take everything in stride.**

There are three ways we can handle these situations:

1. We can sit aside and watch our relatives and loved ones gathering around to enjoy homemade meals, cookies and treats, as we sit with our protein bar, shake, or grilled chicken breast – feeling left out.

2. We can substitute our free day with the holiday or birthday and enjoy all the food we want and then get back on our goals the next day.

3. Or, we can just **take it in stride** and enjoy the day – the food, the company, and the occasion. I have been through this on a few occasions and I recommend the last two

suggestions. It makes things a lot easier, and you won't offend any relatives who worked hard to make such great meals and treats.

I recommend for events such as birthdays and the like, that you make use of suggestion number two and simply replace your free day with the birthday, etc. No harm, no foul.

For other holidays such as Christmas especially, I would recommend suggestion number three. The holiday season comes around once a year, and to be honest with you, I eat more than I should – but I do it guilt free. After those few days are over, I get right back on track. And you will too. The key is to get back into it right away, and not make excuse after excuse to never return.

Eat. Drink. Be merry. And move on.

My dad has some great advice when it comes to this time of year. He says, "It's not what you eat between Thanksgiving and New Year's that really matters. It's what you eat between New Year's and Thanksgiving that does."

Very good advice, indeed!

OVERDOING IT

You will get to a point where you're feeling awesome about your results. You wake up every day ready to workout and take charge. This is a good thing. But one thing I want you to be cautious of is overdoing it. This happens when you work out too much, or go for a long time, never having a day where you eat whatever you want.

You might think that if you eat even less and exercise even more, you will lose weight faster and reach your goals in record time. While it may be true that you lose weight faster, you will be doing your body no good by taking this approach. I must confess that even I fell prey to this line of thinking, and let me tell you, it can set you back weeks, even months.

What happened to me is this: I was working out twice a day, lifting weights in the morning and at night, and then running after my evening weight workout. I did this six days a week, and then ran the seventh day. Initially, I felt good. But after a few weeks, I began to lose energy – **a lot of**

energy. I no longer looked forward to my workouts, I craved sweets worse than before, and I began to binge eat.

The problem was that I was not allowing my body to get the rest it needed, and because I was not feeding it properly, and **not actually eating enough**, I was getting weaker. I kept wondering why I wasn't getting the six-pack abs I wanted (I was doing over 1,000 crunches a day), and why my body still looked "soft," with little muscle definition.

As I did more research and reading, I found out that I was working out so much that my body was using muscle for fuel instead of body fat or carbohydrates. In a way, I was taking one step forward and three steps back. I was thin, but I had no energy and was losing muscle. It was all mental.

Eventually, I had to force myself to limit my workouts to one a day, and then eventually to lifting three days a week and doing cardio three days a week and resting one day. This wasn't easy, and at times I felt guilty for not doing more, but in the long run, I felt better, had more energy, and I gained some needed muscle back. I even started to see my abs!

A FEW WORDS ON ABS

Here's a quote I want you to remember if you're looking to gain six pack abs and have some definition in your midsection to show at the beach or pool.

"Abs come from your diet, exercise."

As I mentioned before, I used to do 1,000 crunches or sit-ups per day – and I still wasn't getting the results I wanted. In the end, what I had to focus on was what I was putting into my stomach, not how I was exercising it. When it comes to abs, your most important "workout" is going to be what you eat.

Train your abs as you would any other body part. Would you do 1,000 squats or bench presses? Nonsense. Why should your abs be any different? Besides, your body loses weight in equal amounts throughout your whole body. **There is no such thing as spot reducing** – meaning that you can't lose weight from only one area. You'll lose weight gradually everywhere.

For men, since their center of gravity is their waistline, more fat tends to concentrate in this area. That's why, if you're male, it may seem that you're not losing the weight from your stomach as quickly as you would like. Factors such as stress will also lead to a bigger stomach on guys.

For women, their center of gravity is in their hip region. It's much easier for their body to store fat here than anywhere else. If it appears you're losing weight everywhere else except your stomach or hips, don't worry. It is coming off. It's just concentrated more in those areas.

Don't get discouraged when you don't see abs immediately. They will come. I promise!

Finally, I don't want you to think that your success is determined by your abs showing up. Your goal doesn't have to be getting a "six-pack". If it is, fine, but if it isn't that's ok too.

ALCOHOL AND TOBACCO

When it comes to vices, I put these two at the top for setting you back in your gains. If you're a heavy beer or liquor drinker, you may want to consider cutting back – a lot.

There's little nutritional value in alcohol. Try to limit it to your weekly "cheat day" if you can, and even on that day, **don't over-consume**. There might be some of you asking, "What about all I hear about the benefits of red wine?" It is true that there are benefits to your health in drinking a glass of red wine now and then.

This doesn't give you license to booze it up on that merlot or cabernet you have sitting around. One glass every now and again is fine. Too much will set you back. After all, they're called "beer bellies" for a reason.

If you're a habitual smoker, you may want to consider quitting by taking a stop-smoking course. Smoking can and will set you back. You'll find it's hard to do any sort of workout, let alone intense cardio. **Consider quitting today**.

THE LOW CARB CRAZE

There has been a lot of speculation on whether the low carb diet is beneficial to our health. Let me give a few details as to why I think it can be both helpful and hurtful.

To begin, it can be helpful purely because it teaches people to avoid processed sugars, refined carbohydrates, and white flour products. It also helps people avoid overeating carbohydrates that can cause rapid fat gain. It teaches people to focus on good sources of fat and protein and eating healthy fruits and vegetables.

The hurtful thing about low carb dieting is that people take it way too far. There are advocates that claim you can eat all the fat, sausages, cheese, and meats that you want. If you're not eating carbohydrates, you're ok.

This isn't the case. Overeating is overeating no matter which foods you use to do it with. Granted, protein raises your body's metabolism, but if you over-consume anything, you're still going to gain weight. Period. We must remember that everything needs to be in balance. Additionally, consideration should be made for the **quality** of protein and fat. In other words, not all protein is good, not all fat is good.

In the nutrition and exercise portion of this program, I provide a useful guide as to what foods you should be focusing on – and which to avoid. From there, you can modify your diet to fit your tastes based on what you learn.

AN UNSTABLE PYRAMID

Some advice I want you to avoid is that of the USDA when it comes to their food pyramid. To me, this is one of the reasons why more and more people in the United States are overweight and obese. If you look at the pyramid, you'll notice it's built on a foundation of carbohydrates: 6-11 servings per day!

Of course, that begs the question, **"What is a serving?"**

Typically, a serving is going to consist of roughly the size of your clenched fist or the palm of your hand – give or take a little bit. That doesn't seem like a lot, but with 6-11 servings, that's still too much, especially when it's the base, and the backbone of the pyramid. In today's world of super-sizing and bigger portions, 6-11 servings **will make you fat.**

Next, the pyramid recommends 2 servings of fruit and 3 servings of vegetables. Too much fruit can cause an overload of sugar in your system. I do not agree with is what the USDA considers "a fruit serving". They consider canned fruit, dried fruit and even fruit juice to be servings. **Stay away from these!** Canned fruit is almost always floating in sugary syrup, dried fruit has concentrated sugar amounts, and fruit juice is nothing **but** sugar.

When you eat fruit, make sure it's whole, and in portions the size of your clenched fist or palm. You'll benefit from the whole fruit because it holds water, which will hydrate you and fill you up easily. Whole fruit also has fiber, which your body needs, and it's in its most natural state – **the less processed the better. Buy or grow organic if possible.**

With vegetables, you're going to want to eat them in either their raw form, or perhaps lightly steamed. In a pinch, you can eat canned veggies, but try to avoid doing this as they are devoid of much of the nutrients found in raw veggies. Aim to make vegetables the bulk of your carbohydrate portions, as they fill you up, have good amounts of fiber, and hold **great** amounts of essential nutrients such as antioxidants and phytochemicals. Both antioxidants and phytochemicals are cancer-fighting agents. **Again - the less processed the better. Buy or grow organic if possible.**

Next, the pyramid recommends only 2 servings a day from the meat group. This couldn't be further from being correct. Whether grazing or fasting, the main ingredient should **be** protein.

Another often-misunderstood point I want to clarify is that peanuts, beans, peanut butter, and soy products do not count as meat servings and are not quality sources of protein. Yes, they do contain protein; however, the protein they contain is incomplete (not having all the essential amino acids). Without going into too much detail, this simply means that your body is going to have a harder time making muscle out of this that it would beef, chicken, eggs, and other complete proteins containing all the essential amino acids.

The next group is what the USDA calls the dairy group. Although milk can be beneficial for some, I believe it can do more harm than good. The reason being that milk is loaded with a natural sugar called lactose. Too much of this can cause fat gain, not to mention an upset stomach, also called lactose intolerance. Also, with the added risk of chemicals and antibiotics given to the cow, and added to the nutrient-robbing pasteurization process, milk isn't necessarily a healthy choice.

When I have milk, it's usually on my cheat day, when I can have it with a few cookies. Cheese is also in this group. Cheese is a good source of protein, good fat, and enzymes. And no, fried cheese curds do not count. Having been born and raised in Wisconsin this was especially tough for me! Butter is also in this group and is an excellent source of fat. To repeat: **buy organic if possible.**

With sweets, limit them to your cheat day. It's that easy.

FIBER

The jury is out regarding the benefits of fiber, such as aiding in digestion, cleansing the colon, reducing the risk of certain cancers, etc. Like protein, it may give you a full, satisfied feeling when you're eating.

Many fruits and vegetables have good amounts of fiber in them. Do not peel apples or other fruits/vegetables as the bulk of their fiber is in the skin.

High fiber, low-carb tortillas are another excellent source. Stay clear of "fiber drinks" that are loaded with sugar and refined carbohydrates, and of processed foods that claim high fiber.

Read nutrition labels carefully!

READ THE LABEL

When you go to the store and buy food or supplements, please make sure you know what you are buying. Just because something says "all natural" or "wholesome" or "recommended by doctors (or whatever celebrity is pushing the product and getting paid by the company to push it)," doesn't mean that it's any better than the rest of the garbage out there.

Take the time to research the product yourself. When you look at the package, you're going to want to take note of two things:

1. Nutrition Facts and,

2. Ingredients

Under the "nutrition facts," you're going to want to look for the totals of calories, fat, carbohydrates, sugar, fiber, and protein. And whenever possible, non-GMO and organic are preferred.

When you measure out these servings, you don't

have to be counting calories, just portions the size of your fist or palm. You'll be surprised at how the package servings will differ from your servings. Stick with your servings the size of the palm or fist, and you'll be just fine.

Under carbohydrates, you'll find the "subcategory" of sugar. Make sure this as close to zero as possible. Too much sugar, as you already know, is detrimental to your goals.

When it comes to reading the ingredients, be cautious of what is called "all natural". Ingredients such as bleached flour, high fructose corn syrup, corn syrup, and animal byproducts are considered "natural" but are hardly found in nature.

Corn syrup, high fructose corn syrup (HFCS), and other syrups such as these are not found in nature. They are byproducts of corn when it is manipulated with chemicals to produce these sweeteners. **Stay away as they do your body no good** and, in fact, high fructose corn syrup is easily converted into fat by your liver. Since it is cheap to use, HFCS is found in many, many foods. You'll be surprised at how many products out there have HFCS in them. But with due diligence, you'll find nutritious food that is free of it. In fact, **the more you stick to truly natural foods, the better**.

Another byproduct of corn is maltodextrin. This is used in a lot of sugar-free products such as sugar-free gelatin, sugar-free drink mixes, and even in some MRPs (meal replacement powders). Be careful, as it will spike your insulin levels higher than table sugar, white bread, white flour, and even glucose. It's very high on the glycemic index.

The glycemic index is an index of certain foods and their effects on insulin levels. The higher the number out of 100, the higher your insulin levels will raise, causing an increase in fat storage. Maltodextrin is 105 – off the charts! For more information on the glycemic index and the ratings of certain foods, go to primemoverfitness.com.

When you read the list of ingredients, the first ingredients listed are the ones used most heavily in the product. For example, in a can of soda, you'll see water as the first ingredient. Obviously, this is the most used ingredient in the soda. Next is probably HFCS, unless it's diet soda.

Without going into too much detail or getting confusing, know that you should avoid all bleached flour products, including pretzels, white bread, white flour tortillas, etc. Additionally, avoid bleached white rice, partially hydrogenated oils, monosodium glutamate (MSG), dextrose (sugar), and quite frankly, any word that you cannot pronounce or have a hard time pronouncing.

Another thing to look for is any word or combination of words ending in "ose". Chances are any word in the list of ingredients ending in "ose" is a sugar – most likely a chemically derived sugar. **Avoid it**!

If you stick to avoiding "food" with these items in its list of ingredients, you'll have a good start on understanding what you should be buying and eating. When buying meat such as chicken or beef, always buy chicken breasts without the skin, and focus on the lean cuts of beef such as sirloin, and ground round or ground sirloin. Gradually, you can also get into grass-fed meats and diary, as well.

Believe me, **you are what you eat**, just as these animals are what they eat, and what's injected into them. Stick to meats that are fed a diet you're striving to achieve. You will be that much healthier for it. It may cost a little more initially, but your longevity is worth it. As David Yoho says, "If you had a Porsche, you'd fill it with premium."

A STABLE PYRAMID

Now let's talk about a stable pyramid. One of the fundamentals regarding financial planning and saving money revolves around what is known as the financial planning pyramid. You may hear other names such as the wealth management pyramid, the financial house, etc. You may also see different stages or "building blocks" added here or there, but I've broken it down for this book to three basic levels for easier understanding.

The first level is where we see risk management. This is the foundation of your plan. It's important to have a strong base to build off, otherwise the slightest of breezes or tremors can send it toppling.

Risk management can be simply seen as your insurance – and this can range from your auto, home, renters, life, health, disability, and umbrella insurance, to your will, emergency fund, and debt management. The reason why insurance is the base is due to the fact that we have risks that most of us cannot afford to take on ourselves. Most of us don't have $300,000 stored away to rebuild our home if it's destroyed and most of us don't have a million dollars to pay in case were liable for damages in an auto accident. By using proper risk management and having the correct insurance in place, we can leverage that risk and only pay a small amount of premium for a large amount of coverage. The proper insurance coverage will make sure in the event of the worst happening, you have a bad day, not a bad life. Proper coverage can protect our wealth and our savings. Likewise, with an emergency fund and a will. An emergency fund is just that – 3 to 6 months of living expenses in case you lose your job, become ill or suffer a loss and have high insurance deductibles. A will protects you by making sure when you die, your possessions go to the people you want them to and assign guardians for your children.

The next level is the wealth accumulation level. This is where we start saving via IRAs, 401(k)s, and other savings vehicles. It may also be the area where you may invest in not only the stock market, but also real estate, and other investments you know. Notice that it builds off the risk management foundation – just in case you're sued or suffer a catastrophic loss, your wealth is secure, since you have a solid base. Make sense?

Finally, you have the estate planning level making the pyramid complete. This is where distributions strategies are employed regarding the wealth you've built, where proper trusts and other legal entities are employed to protect wealth from taxation. It's also the level where people think about charitable giving and leaving a legacy.

It goes without saying; please see a competent professional when working and employing strategies in any of the levels of the pyramid.

SOME FINAL THOUGHTS

Before you get started on your road to health and wealth, I recommend you see your doctor and get a complete physical check-up. At the very least, your doctor will be able to inform you of any problems you may have and give you any warnings you need to hear.

Of course, this program does not attempt to replace expert medical advice but **be cautious of who you take your nutritional information from**. I have a hard time taking advice from people not living the example – including doctors. I'm not saying doctors are ignorant when it comes to nutritional advice but check their credentials if you're unsure of the advice they give you.

Don't be afraid to ask questions, and if you don't get the right answers, just check the doctor's waistline – that will give you plenty of information.

As you would your physical health, I recommend you get a financial check-up, as well. Check your credit for flaws or anomalies. Talk to your financial planner or your wealth manager – **find out what they do – and if it's working**. Most importantly, gain as much information as possible on money and how it can work for you. Take the time to learn about what you're saving or investing in. Don't just take someone's word for it.

Remember, there's a **big difference** between a fiduciary and a salesperson. The difference in knowing is going to depend on your own knowledge as well, so get smart before you get scammed.

Read as much as you can about health and money. It's your life, it's your health, and it's your money. Why not figure out how to live long enough, and healthy enough to enjoy the money you will have? If you find something that works, or when you have success, drop me an email at **sterling.raskie@gmail.com** and let me know – I'd be happy to hear from you!

LOSE WEIGHT, SAVE MONEY

FITNESS AND NUTRITION PLAN

This plan will focus on three main ingredients to losing fat and gaining mass quickly over the course of your journey. These ingredients are:

- INTENSE TRAINING
- PROPER DIET AND NUTRITION
- REST

I encourage you to read this section over and over and over until its concepts and principles become almost second nature to you. Print out a few copies to have with you and read it at work, before you go to bed, while you're relaxing, and when you get up in the morning. It is vital to have a complete understanding of what you're doing and what you need to do to get started on the right track. It will also insure good habits from the start.

As you already know, weight training is simply the best way to put on lean muscle. In this program, you will be focusing on lifting weights that are not impossible for you, but that aren't a cakewalk, either. The main key to success in this program is **consistency** and **intensity**. Try your *hardest* not to miss a workout or a meal. Focus on the negative part (slowly lowering the weight) of the lifts and over time you *will* see a difference. Your body will reward you with excellent results if you stay true to yourself, the program and your goals.

Which brings us to our next issue: GOALS.

If you want more insight into goal setting, I highly recommend Brian Tracy's book, <u>*Goals!*</u>

To begin write out five fitness goals that you would like to achieve throughout the course of this program. Make sure you study them carefully and write down *reasonable* goals. What I mean by this is that it's important not to set a goal so high that you can't possibly achieve it. For example, if I wrote down a goal stating that I'd like to be able to bench-press 2000 pounds; that would be a goal that's too high. Instead, I might write down 300 lbs. This goal is sensible and attainable, yet not so easy that I'll do it in a matter of days.

You want to lose weight. Set a reasonable amount you want to lose (2-3 lbs. per week is ideal). That goal can and will be attainable.

Make sure you write down five goals and read them every night before you go to bed and every morning when you get up - WITHOUT FAIL.

Next, write down three positive and negative affirmations. In the book, *The Secrets of Super Selling,* the authors recommend that you first tell your mind what *not* to do, followed by exactly what to do. For example, if your goal was to lose weight, you might say, "Losing weight is not hard for me. Losing weight is easy for me." "I lose two pounds per week."

Also, always write your goals in the first person, present tense. This programs your subconscious to take action immediately in the "here and now."

Write down your specific goal(s) (i.e. whatever weight, shape, athletic goal you want to attain). You can also put up a photo of someone whose physique you'd like to achieve and of someone you don't ever want to look like. Keep these photos where you can see them every day (the fridge is always good). This will help keep you motivated and act as a sweet/negativity deterrent more than you know.

Once you've reached a certain goal, reward yourself!! This can be that new toy you've had your eye on, or something you've denied yourself until you reached that goal. ***Do not reward yourself with food!*** A "cheat" day is not a reward, but part of the program itself!!

Finally, sign and date your goals. Giving yourself a deadline and committing to it with your signature produces a sense of urgency and importance. After all, can you think of anything you sign that *isn't* important? Think of it as a contract obligation to yourself!

Before we get into the swing of lifting, cardio and the routine and program I will lay out for you, we must talk about one of the most, if not *the* most important part of your program: DIET AND NUTRITION. **You will not get the results you want without it**.

This is very important. Since your main concern is to cut some weight, you need to eat more, yes *more*. Your metabolism is a little slow right now, and to lose weight (body fat) you need to create a *slight* calorie deficit in your body. And this means eating good, quality foods, and not junk foods (you'll have to control your sweet tooth for a while!).

5-6 small meals a day are what we're shooting for here. If you want to lose weight, you're going to have to make your body digest and assimilate calories more efficiently. You should aim for a daily calorie intake of 12 times to 13 times your bodyweight in calories. This can easily be done by measuring portions of protein with the size of your palm, and carb portions the size of your clenched fist. This is a simple rule of thumb.

The main ingredient that builds muscle and the *only* one that can build muscle *and* burn fat is PROTEIN. I cannot emphasize this enough. Protein is the only thing that will build muscle. Fat won't do it, and neither will carbs. Carbs and fats simply give you the energy you need to live and exercise, and the lubrication your bones and joints need to function, as well as the fats you need for proper brain function and maintenance (almost all of your brain is fat!).

As you already know, protein is made up of **amino acids** It's these little things of beauty that repair your damaged muscle tissue after an intense workout. Good sources of protein include beef, cheese, chicken, pork, turkey, and of course, supplements such as protein drinks. Stick to these

quality sources of protein, as they are the best for your body.

The following pages include some guidelines on what consists of good foods, foods that you should consider limiting or avoiding all together, and foods you can eat to your heart's content.

Do's and Don'ts

MUST HAVES

- Protein
- Good fats (cheese, butter, coconut oil, olive oil)
- Fiber
- Water
- Vitamins B, C, D
- Rest (8-10 hours of sleep a night)
- Some cooking
- "Cheat" day/meal every week
- Staying focused
- Writing down your goals
- Positive attitude

Do's and Don'ts

DO NOTS!

- Trans fats

- Simple carbs

- Carbs before bed

- Seed Oils

- Bleached flour

- High fructose corn syrup (and all foods containing it!)

- Soy

- Negativity

Foods That Help

PROTEIN

- Chicken

- Turkey

- Eggs

- Cheese

- Venison/wild game/fish

- Grass-fed beef, poultry, or wild game

Foods That Help

CARBOHYDRATES

- Broccoli
- Green, leafy vegetables
- Carrots
- Celery
- Cauliflower
- Home grown garden vegetables

I also keep chickens and a garden which allows me to get fresh eggs and vegetables.

FATS

Your body needs fat to lose weight and to function properly.

Good sources of fat include Omega 3, 6, and 9 as they are all essential fatty acids (EFAs). They can be monounsaturated, polyunsaturated, or saturated.

Never cook with polyunsaturated fats as they turn into trans-fats very easily from breaking down in high heat. Extra virgin coconut oil is a great choice, and your body will not store it as fat, even though it is a saturated fat. Trust me. More information on fats can be found in Udo Erasmus' book, *Fats That Heal, Fats That Kill.*

* Do not use <u>any</u> trans fats such as vegetable shortening or margarine. Do not use any seed oils. These are very bad for you!

Foods That Help

GOOD FATS

- Olive oil
- Coconut oil
- Butter
- Fish oil
- Cheese
- Egg yolks
- Nuts*

Nuts: Dry roasted or raw. Don't use honey roasted, or nuts roasted in any other oils. The ingredients should read: (nut of choice), with or w/out salt. Nuts are best consumed in moderation but are good sources of essential fats and can calm hunger pangs that lead to binge eating.

- Almonds
- Pecans
- Cashews
- Sunflower Seeds
- Walnuts
- Macadamia
- Other good sources of fats are olives

<u>*Free Foods*</u>

(Enjoy as much of these as you want!)

- Herbs and spices
- Sugar-free gum
- Coffee (black)
- Tea (Unsweetened)
- Club soda/sparkling water
- Water
- Vinegars

EATING

This is where you'll see the biggest difference in the shortest amount of time. Your eating habits will be the hardest to change and stick to, but I know you can do it. Start gradually into your eating program, and you will soon become accustomed to it. You'll never want to go back.

Allow yourself a "cheat" day/meal once a week, without guilt or worry. This will help prevent binges and eating a ton of sweets. "Cheat" days, or free days, as I have heard them called, are quite necessary to your fitness goals. These days, one per week, allow you to still feel human and enjoy some of the pleasures in life.

Personally, I love these days. And it's not uncommon for me to throw down a whole pizza followed by a half-gallon of ice cream for dessert. Hey, it only comes once a week, so I go for the gusto! You might feel a little hesitant on your first "cheat" day. You might not even cheat that much. But that hesitancy will be long forgotten on your second or third "cheat" day. They really do work and help me to stay the course for the week, knowing that I can indulge on that one day – guilt free!

Eating habits are tricky and often difficult to change. You're going to be making adjustments that you and your body will not be used to. That's ok. Just start small and take it one meal at a time. Remember that a habit takes 30 to 60 days to break and change, so you **can** do this, it just takes time.

If you find yourself in a real pinch and craving a load of sweets, drink a big glass of water. This will especially help to prevent cravings later at night, or at any time for that matter. The urge will last a short time, so get through that. But allow yourself to indulge now and then. That's what "cheat" days are for!

Whether intermittent fasting or grazing, body will get used to it. Your body will also need vital nutrients, protein, carbs, and fats lost during your intense workouts, and must be replenished to speed recovery.

Eat when hungry and until you are satisfied, not until you're full or "stuffed". Don't eat any carbs late in the day or, heaven forbid, at night. Most of your calories should come from protein, followed by complex/fibrous carbs and good fats.

If you still feel somewhat hungry after you're done eating, drink a glass of water or two. Also, if you eat more fiber, you'll feel fuller, since it's just bulk and not high in calories. **But you must eat; your metabolism depends on it**. Eating more protein and fat makes you feel hungry less often.

WEIGHT TRAINING

Three days per week. Do cardio on alternate days. Rest one day.

We've now gotten to the point where you need to know what lifts will help you the most, and how many sets and reps to do. First, let's start with the most basic lifts that will help you. These can be classified as **compound lifts**, as they work a vast majority of muscles at the same time. These are the kind of exercises that will help you trim. You needn't focus on elaborate machines or focus on one exercise for one specific muscle. Leave that to the Mr. Olympia's and the pro bodybuilders.

<u>You must primarily use free weights or your own weight!</u> Using free weights or your own weight will help you gain more muscle, show your true strength, and build vital stabilizer muscles that aid in helping the main muscle lift the weight (since you have to keep balance while you lift).

NOTE: Form is of utmost importance when lifting weights and exercising. Proper form means better, quicker, and safer results. Stand in front of a mirror while you are lifting so that you can watch yourself to make sure you're doing the lifts correctly.

I would much rather have you start with lighter weights and proper form, than heavy weights and sacrifice proper form and risk injury. Consequently, you'll be doing yourself no good by "cheating" when you lift. You're just cheating yourself. Everybody starts somewhere. Don't be embarrassed when you go to the gym and you're lifting lighter weights at first. I did the same thing, and I'm glad I did. In this way, you'll get faster results. You'll be surprised at how sore you'll be from using what looked to be "easy" weight.

When you lift, focus not only on form, but also on squeezing (flexing) your muscles at the top of the lift for a count of 1. **Remember that you should have a count of 1 on the concentric (positive) part of the lift, and a count of 2 on the eccentric (negative) part of the lift** For example, if you were doing dumbbell curls, you'd curl the weight and count "1" and then hold it there and squeeze (making a muscle) for a count of "1". And then lower the weight for a count of

"2" (meaning it should take you 2 seconds to lower the weight).

NOTE: It is the eccentric (negative) part of the lift that will cause the most stress on muscles leading to growth. That's why it's important that you focus on the negative (lowering of the weight or body).

Always remember to get a good night's sleep after exercising. Your muscles grow while you REST, not during the workout.

Stretching is a good idea. This helps prime your muscles and body for the stress you're about to put it through, warming up muscles and helping prevent injury. It will also help you recover quicker from workouts.

A SPECIAL NOTE TO WOMEN:

You **WILL NOT** gain an exorbitant amount of muscle mass. Many women are concerned that once they start exercising, strength training or weight lifting that they will "bulk up". This just isn't true. While you will gain some muscle mass which is good, and it will help you increase your metabolism and burn more calories even while resting, in order to obscenely and unhealthily pack on the muscle, you'd have to be eating an extreme amount of calories and or using steroids.

Since you'll be eating less, you simply won't be getting the calories needed to really bulk up. Additionally, your body just isn't equipped to deliver as much testosterone as your male counterparts. Relax. You're not going to bulk up but adding a few pounds of muscle in exchange for fat is a *good* thing.

COMPOUND EXERCISES

Bench Press (pectorals, triceps, deltoids): This lift will predominantly build your chest. Your triceps will get a good workout as well as your shoulders.

Push-Ups (pectorals, triceps, deltoids): If you don't have weights or can't get to the gym, these are excellent. I still do them. These are also good if you're away on business or vacation.

Overhead Presses (deltoids, triceps): This lift will really blast your shoulders.

Pull-Ups/Rows (back, biceps, abs): These are great and some of my favorites for building my lats and biceps! Don't scoff at these. When done right, these exercises and lifts will cause great gains and soreness. Don't worry if you can only do 1 or 2 when you first start. You'll gradually increase.

Squats/Deep Knee Bends (quads, lower back): A lift for building big quads and leg mass. Also, these will help give you that explosive boost and power on the track, or help to strengthen muscles for jumping you may not have used for a long time, and that need to be rebuilt. These are also good for dunking a basketball! **Always remember to keep good form**.

Deadlifts (hamstrings, back, deltoids): Great lift for your hamstrings and back.

Dips (deltoids, triceps, pectorals): I love these. I usually do anywhere from 4 sets to failure (until you can do no more) or one set to failure as a finale to my chest/upper body workout. When done correctly and focusing on the negative, you won't be able to do many, but you will get a great stretch, a good pump of blood to the muscles, and fantastic gains!

You will work your upper body two days a week and your lower body one day. For example, when you begin on a Monday, Wednesday and Friday program, you will work your upper body on Monday and Friday and save your lower body workout for Wednesday. This way your body is getting a complete all-around workout, which is necessary to your success.

Choose two exercises for each muscle group and do 5 sets of one and then a burnout set for another. For example, I might do 5 sets of bench presses ranging from 15 reps (warm up), to 10 reps (heavier) for my final lift on the fourth set. Then on the fifth set, I reduce the weight and do as many reps as I can. Immediately after that lift, I go to 1 set of 10-15 reps of dumbbell flyes or even push-ups.

This is how a workout should pan out: Warm up with lighter weight and do one set. Then rest for 1-2 minutes between sets (**this is important since your workouts should be between 30 and 60 minutes, or less**). Do another set with heavier weight and so on. Then, when you are finished with the fifth set of bench presses (the burnout set) go immediately to the dumbbell flyes or push-ups. Do this for all your lifts and exercises. Simply choose two exercises you want to do and make one your major set and the other your minor set. You can also do 4 sets of 12 reps each for a change of pace.

Remember to use weight that is challenging, but NEVER sacrifice form.

NO EQUIPMENT NECESSARY

If you're nervous about getting started or concerned that you don't have the right tools and equipment to get the job done, don't worry. You're not alone. While weights and equipment can be beneficial and helpful, they aren't necessary. I have a small set of dumbbells and a small curl bar that I use occasionally to change up my routine. If I am traveling, I take advantage of the hotel's gym and weights. But most of my workouts are done at home, at a park, or a playground. Some of the best exercises you can do can be done quick, and free. Push-ups, crunches, pull-ups, squats, jumping rope and sprints can be done from the comfort of your home while watching TV or at the local park or playground if the weather is nice. Well isn't that something – we just eliminated another excuse!

I would easily double your reading by including explanations and how-to's for each exercise. To see examples and demonstrations on what certain exercises are and how to do them, feel free to do an Internet search or type in the exercise name in YouTube. That should more than help you get started with an understanding of which exercise does what.

Upper Body

Chest

- Push-Ups
- Barbell Bench Press
- Barbell Incline Bench Press
- Dumbbell Bench Press
- Dumbbell Incline Bench Press
- Dumbbell Flyes
- Cable Crossovers

Shoulders

- Dumbbell Press
- Overhead Press
- Front Raises
- Lateral Raises
- Reverse Flyes
- Upright Cable Rows
- Upright Barbell Rows

Back

- Pull-Ups
- Lat Pulldowns
- One-Arm Dumbbell Rows
- Seated Cable Rows
- Back Extensions

Biceps

- Dumbbell Curls
- Barbell Curls
- Preacher Curls
- Concentration Curls
- Cable Curls
- Hammer Curls

Triceps

- Seated Triceps Presses
- Lying Triceps Presses
- Triceps Kickbacks
- Triceps Pushdowns
- Cable Extensions
- Bench Dips

Lower Body

Quadriceps

- Barbell Squats
- Leg Presses
- Leg Extensions

Hamstrings

- Dumbbell Lunges
- Straight-Leg Deadlifts
- Lying Leg Curls

Calves

- Jumping Rope
- Seated Calf Raises
- Standing Heel Raises

Abs

- Floor Crunches
- Oblique Floor Crunches
- Hanging Knee Raises
- Reverse Crunches
- Cable Crunches
- Decline Crunches

CARDIO

First and foremost, if your primary concern is losing body fat, consider doing your exercising in the morning *before* breakfast. You have a greater chance to **burn more body fat** in the morning after an overnight fast (sleeping without eating) than any other time of day! Also, try not to eat at least an hour after cardio, as your body will still be "doing cardio" and burning off body fat even after you've finished. And since you have no energy stores in your muscles from your overnight fast, your body has no choice but to burn excess body fat for fuel!

You can do your cardio for anywhere from 10 to 20 minutes on alternate days to your lifting days: 3 days lifting, 3 days cardio, rest on Sundays. I like to lift on Mondays, Wednesdays, and Fridays, do cardio on Tuesdays, Thursdays, and Saturdays, and rest and have my "Cheat" day on Sunday.

As with lifting, you must make your cardio intense. But again, start small, and work your way up. For example, you can warm up for two to three minutes simply by walking. Then, every minute thereafter, turn up the speed just a little. Do that every 5 minutes for a 20-minute cardio session and every 6 minutes for a 30-minute cardio session. You can also do sprinting intervals in which you sprint for a short distance and walk for a short distance.

Now, my all-out sprint (maximum intensity) will be different than yours, of course. The main idea is to push yourself for those 20 or 30 minutes (you should be sweating pretty good). The beauty of this is that you never reach a plateau, and you're constantly striving and pushing yourself further and further. And you can mix it up if you'd like. You can use a treadmill, or do the same cycle on an exercise bike, running, swimming, etc.

You might have to get up earlier to do your cardio or lift. Eat a good quality breakfast with a portion of protein and carbs when your cardio is completed. Just remember to wait for one hour before chowing down. Hey, why not take the time to prepare a delicious meal?

There are different variations to cardio. You can do moderate intensity for 20-30 minutes on a treadmill, bike, or running. Don't feel you have to go out and buy weights or cardio equipment. When I was overweight and lost 65 pounds, all I used was myself!

One cardio routine that has helped me has been High Intensity Interval Training or HIIT. This consists of a warm up period, and then a series of sprints and brief rests, then a cool down period. Also, **don't be afraid to do a fun sport or activity that involves cardio**. I play basketball quite a bit, sometimes for a few hours at a time. It's a great way to do cardio and I'm having fun too! Other times, my workout is fighting a current and the terrain when I'm trout fishing or hiking or walking in the woods. Get your whole family involved! Kids can learn good habits from you, their hero, and having the whole family working and playing with you is a great way to bond and make this more fun!

SUPPLEMENTS

Supplements can help you along your way to your goals. They can be convenient when looking for a quick meal of quality protein, carbs, and fats, as well as aid in recovery. However, ***they are not magic***, and they do not work without proper diet and exercise. You can, and will, get results without them. Here's a list of what I use or have used to help me:

- Whey Protein (meal replacement)

- Vitamin C (immune system)

- Vitamin D

- Multi-vitamin

- Calcium

- Vitamin B Complex (energy)

I suggest before you buy anything, that you do your homework and read up on any you might think of taking. Many of these supplements can be found at health food stores or on the web.

DON'T GET CAUGHT UP IN THE DIET PILL HYPE! YOU WILL GET RESULTS WITHOUT THEM!

This is just a blueprint to help get you going. You can customize it to fit your tastes (food wise) but stick to the workouts and the guide to the lifts, foods, and the like. And if anytime you feel like you're losing motivation, stop and think for a moment. Why quit? You can always quit, so why quit now? You can do it! And I congratulate you on your desire to change and succeed!

LOSE WEIGHT, SAVE MONEY

FINANCIAL PLAN

10 Ways to Boost your Credit Score

Credit score. What the heck is it and how did I ever get one in the first place? The truth is, when you first started out in life, your score was 0; a clean slate –fresh, free, and naïve. When I started out, I was the same way. I had a score of 0. And my financial IQ was just the same. As I got older, I learned the hard way. I bought things on credit, struggled to pay the bills, made excuses, got angry and placed blame on this person or that company for "selling" me this or that. I thought the best way to snub them was to not pay the bill. I was way wrong! The only person I was hurting was me. And my credit score.

Your credit score is a number that is assigned to you (or you and your spouse if you're married) based on how many items you have purchased on credit (and you're making payments on) and the schedule at which you've made payments (how many payments you have made, the amount you're paying on, and the timeliness of the payment).

Credit ranges anywhere from the low 300s (considered poor credit history or high risk) to the mid-800s (considered great credit history or low risk). Some people have no credit at all. This could be people who've used cash to pay for everything or new immigrants who are brand new to this country, to a newly graduated high school teen, on their way to college. If you aren't already, you should aim to be in the 650 to 800 range.

And there's no reason why you shouldn't.

There has never been a greater need to be conscious of your finances and how you spend your money than there is today. Every day we are bombarded with the "next best thing" or the hottest new car or truck or the latest and greatest gadget. The list of things we want to buy or think we need is endless.

Too often we are sucked into the trap of the keeping up with the Jones' mentality. The next-door neighbor just got a huge big screen TV with surround sound to watch the game on and you're left with your old 30 inch box with its built-in speakers. Or you go to visit a friend's house and not only is there home brand new, but there's a new sedan in the garage, a hot tub out back, and new furniture so comfortable that your friends can't imagine how they lived like barbarians without it.

And you think to yourself, "I work hard." "I should be able to enjoy the same things that they enjoy too!" Your friends and neighbors all seem happy. They all seem to be doing just fine and you begin to wonder why on earth can't you have the same things? So you head to the mall and begin shopping. Blinded by the urge for "want", and ignoring the question, "Do I really *need* this?" Immediately upon entering the store you're bombarded by salespeople asking you what you want, showing you how you can "save" money by upgrading to this or that package, and when you're on the fence about making a decision, they give you an offer you can't refuse – 0% financing!

You buy.

You decide to have a get together to show off your newly acquired goods. You get lots of compliments, pats on the back, and a few "I wish I had…" You feel good about your purchase. And why shouldn't you? You're not even making payments on them yet! Indeed, life is good.

After a few months of "living in luxury" you receive your first bill. But it's not the only bill you receive that month, you also have rent, utilities, and groceries to buy – something that slipped your mind when you were mesmerized by the bright lights and big sounds of your purchase. Suddenly you feel a bit of buyer's remorse. You feel a little worried and concerned when you look at your checkbook and realize that there's not enough to go around. You start to prioritize. You have to pay rent. You *need* a roof over your head. You *have* to have electricity and a phone. You *need* to eat.

You tell yourself that it's ok to be a little late on your first payment.

You figure you get paid in another week, and you can use that money to make your first payment. After all, who's going to notice that you're only a few days late on your payment?

You continue and follow through with your plan. Until it backfires.

While driving to work you get a flat tire. You have to get it fixed since you have to keep working and have to go back and forth to work. Then some friends ask you to go out to eat with them the following weekend. You think you shouldn't, but what harm could it be to go out and visit? After all you work hard all week. You tell yourself you won't spend a dime.

And you don't – you spend $50!

And on the way home from your outing your gas tank is touching 'E'. You *have* to have gas to drive – so $45 later your tank is at 'F'.

You find yourself scrambling to find the money to make that first payment for your new toys. You begin to regret the purchase, but still tell yourself that you'll make the payment by the end of the month. – still within the grace period.

Through a lot of sweat and worry, you finally make the payment. It's late, but you feel good since you still made it.

And then it happens. It's that time again. The beginning of the month comes. Rent, utilities, and food are due again. You look in your checkbook and realize the money you had for rent is there, but you'll either have to live in the dark and cold or starve. You decide to eat ramen noodles for a while.

Then you get a call from the store you bought your toys from. According to them, you were a few days late with your payment. You kindly remind them that you have the 0% financing plan. And they kindly remind you that even though you're making no *interest* payments, you still have to make those payments on time – and they called to inform you that you must pay a late fee of 15%.

How are you going to pay that?

But alas! Out of nowhere a brand new, clean shiny credit card comes in the mail! Neglecting to read the interest rate that comes with the card, you immediately call to activate it. Your balance is $2,000 - enough to pay off your bill, and plenty to upgrade your car stereo, and take your friends out for a night on the town.

After all, you want them to think you're doing great – making money and enjoying the joie de vivre. You do a great job fooling them.

And now the downward spiral continues. Only this time your rent payment is late, you miss your utilities payment, and you can't even come close to attempting to pay on your toys. And your credit card is maxed out.

As you get deeper and deeper in trouble, your credit score follows you.

And your phone just won't stop ringing. Isn't it funny, you probably never received one phone call from the salesperson following up to make sure everything was ok? After all, they got their commission, why should they care?

However, if you don't pay your bill on time, guess who comes calling? And at the worst possible times. Morning, noon, dinnertime…

Now you're afraid to answer the phone, and you've disguised your voice so many times you forgot who you were the last time they called. It's not a good situation to be in.

But there is hope.

You *can* improve your score and get back on the side of "good standing" with creditors. By following these 10 *easy* steps, you will be on your way to boosting your score and in control of your finances.

1. **Find Out Your Credit Score**

The first thing you need to do is find out what your score is. You can't improve your score unless you know where it's at. This is very easy since you are allowed one free credit report annually. There are three major credit bureaus that you can get your report from, and all of them will be close to each other in terms of your score, give or take a few points. Once you get your score and your report, examine it *thoroughly*. You're going to want to make sure the information on there is accurate and up to date. Check for items that you are currently or have made payments on in the past, and also check for the timeliness of the payments as well. Payments made on time will have a '1' next to them. A '2','3, '4', or'5 will follow payments made late. The numbers correspond to a key that identifies the numbers in order of lateness, 30, 60, or over 90 days past due. Check to make sure that these are accurate and if they're not, call the company to dispute them.

You'll also want to check for fraud. This could mean that someone had used your credit or name to purchase items without your permission – also known as Identity Theft. It could also mean that someone put a false statement on your report without you knowing. If this is the case, call all three of the credit bureaus and put a fraud alert on your report. It's free and it protects you from fraud. What it will also do is freeze your credit, which means if you apply for a loan or credit of any kind, the credit bureaus will call you to make sure it's you who's applying for the credit, and not a thief.

This happened to me with a rather *sly* landlord. He put items on my report that I had never done and made claims that I didn't pay him for repairs. After checking my report, months later, I found that he had put those false items on my report. That same day I called the credit bureaus and put a fraud alert on them. The bureaus worked with me and removed the claim. What I also found out is that a loan that I had was being reported twice. I called the bureaus and let them know I had one loan and not two. Every little bit helps. And in today's world, you must be vigilant when it comes to your financial wellbeing.

A list of the three major credit bureaus with their respective contact information will be in your report and at the end of this section.

2.   Improve Your Credit Score Before You Buy

This may sound a little confusing at first, but as you read further, it will make perfect sense. How do you improve your credit score before you buy? You need to think about your buying decision before you buy. What this means is that you must consider all the things that you are currently paying for. This means mortgage, rent, utilities, groceries, incidentals, car, truck, boat, etc. If you think you're already paying for enough items through monthly payments, it might be in your best interest to determine if what you're thinking on purchasing next is an actual *need* or a *want*. Think about your possible purchase will affect you in 1 year, 3 years, or even 10 years. Will you still be paying on it? Will it still hold the value you're placing on it now? Will it even be worth what you've paid for it? For example, a new car loses almost 25% of its purchase price the instant you drive it off the lot!

What this boils down to is to really think about your future purchase. If you need to, take a day or even a week or a month to think about your decision. Don't be pressured by fast-talking salespeople or tempted by the "today only" offers. There will always be an exciting offer. In fact, most reputable companies would rather you think through your decision than make a hasty one. After all, if they're worth their salt, they'll want you as a long-term, happy customer.

Something else to consider is that every time you apply for a loan or fill out a credit card application, your credit score is checked, and sometimes lowered. The credit bureaus see too many applications for credit as a sign that you're looking to go on a spending spree and penalize you accordingly. You may not even get the loan or the credit card but guess what – your score has been lowered! It pays to think things through before you buy or apply.

3. Set Your Own Credit Card Limit

If you're brand new to credit and you don't have a credit card or cards, this method can be a great way to get started if you think you might be tempted by too high a credit limit. Go to your local bank or credit union and see if there is a credit card that they offer with a low limit. This could be anywhere from $200-$500. This is a great way to keep yourself in check if you think you might be tempted to spend more. What happens is that you use your card, and if one month you get a little over-zealous and spend more than you thought, there's a limit. The card will be "maxed-out" and you won't be able to spend another dime on it until you pay off the balance or make the minimum monthly payment. You won't be able to use the card for purchases until this is done. This can prevent you from spending more than you make or can afford and will keep the creditors from calling non-stop for payments.

If you already have a card, ask your credit card company to lower your limit if possible. If you really feel the need to have a $5,000 or $10,000 limit, so be it. You know what you need. But don't just keep a limit that high for the sake of having it. The temptation is just too great to spend. If you have a high limit and want to keep it, have the discipline to set your own limit, and never go above it. And if you use your card…

4. Pay Off Your Credit Card Every Month

This is one of the golden rules of credit cards. Have the discipline to pay off your card every single month. If you don't, you open yourself up for a heap of late fees, interest charges and so on. Think about it, you purchase a pair of shoes for $50. You use your card. Shortly afterward your statement comes in the mail and you make the minimum payment. Before you know it, 6 months go by and that $50 pair of shoes has now cost you $80. And the credit card company is elated. This is of course how they make their money.

The main convenience of a credit card is to avoid carrying lots of cash. Some people are brilliant with them being able to finance homes, cars, tuition, etc. They have it down to an exact science, and that topic is for another book at another time.

Credit cards shouldn't be used if you *don't have the cash*. One rule of thumb to remember is this: before you make a purchase, make sure you have the money in your checking or savings to cover what you buy with your card. And pay your card off *completely* every time you receive a statement. If you can't cover the purchase with cash you already have, don't put it on your credit card.

5. Get Current On All Of Your Outstanding Debt

If you have any outstanding debt currently, you need to work adamantly on getting your outstanding debt current. This means forgoing that night out with friend or buying that new pair of shoes or set of clothes or whatever it is you want to buy. You need to get current on your debt. When you do this, the credit bureaus will increase your score. Granted it's ever so slightly, but it's still raised nonetheless. This is crucial for your credit future. When you apply for credit in the future, your last seven years of credit history are going to show up. This means that your bad times are going to show up with your most recent undertaking to get caught up.

When a lender sees that you have made an "honest effort" to pay what you *owe* they are more apt to be lenient when you are applying for another loan. This could be that mortgage lender, car dealer, or whomever. And by honest effort, I mean that you strive to get current and *stay* current. It only helps you.

6. Get Set Up On An Automatic Bill Pay System

This is just good sense even if you already have great credit. Simply go to your bank and ask them how you can get started on an automatic bill pay system Most reputable banks offer this to their members. It works even better if you have direct deposit through your employer. What happens is that you set a time and date for your bills to go out. And voila! They're paid on time every month, often without you even knowing they were due. This is a great system if you're a procrastinator, or you have a hard time remembering which bills are which and when they're due. If you're unable to get direct deposit, do your very best to get into the habit of depositing your check every time you get paid so you can pay your bills on time.

7. Pay Off Your Delinquent (written off) Debt

For some of you, this will not apply, for the rest of you - you know what I'm talking about. But don't worry. You can do it! If you've gotten to the situation where you've had lenders write off your debt and declare a loss (on their end), don't think you've won since they've stopped calling you. You may have won the battle, but you are losing the war. What they have done is written you off. Now without going into a lot of tax jargon, really what they've done is called you a complete loss, and they write you off on their books as "hopeless". Worse yet is now that debt becomes "forgiven" and now becomes income that you'll be taxed on.

Even though they might have stopped calling you, you can rest assured that they will put that loss on your credit report. And that is bad. The next worst thing is a bankruptcy claim being placed on your score.

When you make an effort to repay your old and written off debts, not only are your past lenders happy, but it's the right thing to do. After all you borrowed *their* money. It is your responsibility to repay it – no matter what. Think about it. Have you ever loaned something to someone and have them not pay you back? Didn't leave you with a very good taste in your mouth did it? But even if they came back to you 1, 2 or even 5 years later and made an attempt to pay their debt to you, you'd feel pretty good wouldn't you? And I guarantee that you'd be more than willing to work with them on payments or even forgive the debt. I can't guarantee what a lender would do, but they will work with you. Think of it this way and put yourself in the lender's shoes: How many people call them and ask them if they can make arrangements to send money and repay money owed? It's rare. They will be more than willing to work with you. Just don't blow it by falling off the wagon.

8. Work With The Collection Agency

This may seem like a slap in the face to you, but it can only help you in the long run. And it will help you answer the phone with less stress! You need to work with the collection agency no matter what. They can be your best friends or they can make things really miserable for you. You must remember that the person on the other end of the phone calling you is a human being as well. He or she has a life, a family, children, and plenty of other things to worry about besides your screwed-up credit.

You can bet your bottom dollar that if you get smart with them or give them a hard time, they will make a note of it on their computer, so that the next time either they or a different person calls you, and all of a sudden you want to work with them, they might not give you the time of day. This could mean the difference of getting a decent settlement amount worked out, or at least a decent monthly amount you can handle to start paying back what you owe.

The bottom line is: work with the collection agency. *It's their money you owe!* It will save you a lot of grief, stress, and you might even be able to wipe out that debt even faster if you're just plain nice.

9. Pay Yourself First

I know I am repeating myself here, but it's going to make a lot of sense if you follow it. And that rule is: **Pay Yourself First**. This simple statement comes again from George Clason's book, *The Richest Man in Babylon*. The crux of this statement is to set aside a certain amount of money every paycheck into a savings account, investment account or wherever you can put it into and not touch it for a *long* time.

You may be thinking, "How am I supposed to pay myself first, if I'm up to my eyeballs in debt?" That's a good question. The point of this phrase is not to make you forget about your bills, become even more selfish and not pay what you owe. The point is to give you something that's yours – even if it's only a dollar from every paycheck. When you get into the habit of paying yourself first, a neat and almost magical thing begins to happen. You start to want to save more and more and more. As your little stash grows in value, you'll begin to feel more confident about yourself, and believe it or not, you'll want to spend less, and save more!

Eventually, you'll get to the point where you'll be debt free, or at least current with your most outstanding debt (house, car, education loans), and have a sizeable savings built up. You'll be amazed at the confidence and courage you'll have and the wisdom you'll achieve when it comes to making buying decisions in the future. You'll be well on your way to a more secure financial future.

10. Have Patience

The final point I want to make is to have patience. As the saying goes, "Rome wasn't built in a day." This is true for your credit. If you're like me, it may take a bit to get to a "good" or even "excellent" standing, but it will come. If you follow the steps provided here you'll be well on your way to a more structured and disciplined payment schedule, and a sounder footing on your financial and credit future. You must start now. Start today. Make a conscious decision that you are going to improve your credit score and turn your financial life around. You can do it. Take it one step at a time and you'll be well on your way to achieving what you thought was the impossible.

CREDIT BUREAUS

Equifax - http://www.equifax.com/
To order your report, call: 800-685-1111 or write:
P.O. Box 740241, Atlanta, GA 30374-0241

For Fraud Alerts, call: 800-525-6285 and write:
P.O. Box 740241, Atlanta, GA 30374-0241

Hearing impaired call 1-800-255-0056 and ask the operator to call the Auto Disclosure Line at 1-800-685-1111 to request a copy of your report.

Experian - http://www.experian.com/
To order your report, call: 888-EXPERIAN (397-3742) or write:
P.O. Box 2002, Allen TX 75013

For Fraud Alerts call: 888-EXPERIAN (397-3742) and write:
P.O. Box 9530, Allen TX 75013
TDD: 1-800-972-0322

Trans Union - http://www.transunion.com/
To order your report, call: 800- 888 -4213 or write:
P.O. Box 1000, Chester, PA 19022

For Fraud Alerts call: 800-680-7289 and write:
Fraud Victim Assistance Division, P.O. Box 6790,
Fullerton, CA 92634
TDD: 1-877-553-7803

You may also access your free credit report from
each of the three bureaus at
www.annualcreditreport.com

WHY YOU NEED AN EMERGENCY FUND

You may or may not have heard that it's wise to have an emergency fund. Even if you've heard it, you may not be aware of what it means and why you should have one – and more importantly why you need one. An emergency fund is just that. It's money set aside for a rainy day, an unexpected bump in the road, or for a real emergency or an expense that you haven't specifically planned for. Examples of those unexpected expenses (borderline redundant – I know) include a car accident, disability, storm damage to your home, losing a job, being a victim of theft, etc.

So what makes up an emergency fund? Generally, a good place to start is to have a goal of at least 3 to 6 months of non-discretionary living expenses put away in a relatively liquid account such as a savings, checking or money market account. Non-discretionary living expenses are those that *do not* go away, should you lose your job or the ability to generate income. These expenses would include your mortgage payment, rent, utilities, food, car payment and taxes.

Now comes the easy part.

Simply add up all your non-discretionary living expenses that you have in a month and multiply by 3 and then multiply by 6. This is the amount you'd need to have set aside. For example, if I have a $1,200 mortgage, $400 in groceries per month, and utilities of $300, I would have a total of $1,900 monthly in expenses. Multiply that number by 3 ($5,700) and again by 6 ($11,400) and it looks like I'd need between $5,700 and $11,400 set aside for my emergency fund.

These amounts are not set in stone. The amount you'll need will also depend on your job, your income, and how you're paid. If I'm a tenured college professor making $6,000 monthly, I may only need 3 to 6 months put away. If I'm an executive or CEO of a large company and I make $20,000 monthly, or I'm a commissioned sales person making $10,000 monthly, I may consider having a fund of 9 to 12 months. This would be because there's a good chance of me not being able to find another job at that income level if I were fired or laid off. And generally, as peoples' incomes increase, so do their expenses.

Now comes that hard part – *saving* the money.

It's not that hard, it just takes a bit of planning and discipline you'll be well on your way. You can start by putting away a small sum every week or month – depending on what works for you. This could be $50, $100, or even $500 per month until you've funded account. If you're looking for places to find money consider cutting unnecessary expenses until you've got your emergency fund at 100%. Reduce your phone bill, cut your cable TV costs, and pack your lunch instead of dining out. Notice a pattern? These are all discretionary expenses – those that *can* go away if you want them to.

Your emergency fund can also be used in tandem with your insurance deductibles. Let's say you have low deductibles on your auto insurance and want to save some money. You can simply increase your deductibles and should you need to use your deductible for a claim, you can take from your emergency fund. This is wise especially if you rarely file claims. If you have a disability policy with a 60 day elimination period (time deductible) before benefits start, you can use your emergency fund to help cover the expenses for those 60 days until your benefits begin.

Now that you know what an emergency fund is, it's important to know what it's not. It is not a slush fund to buy toys like a new car, boat, TV, etc. It's not money to play with, gamble with or dip into because "It's only a couple bucks, it can't hurt anything." Those couple of bucks can add up to thousands in no time. Don't steal from yourself. Resist the temptation to spend it. If you feel you may be the type of person to be tempted, consider putting the money in an account that's not easy to get to – such as a money market account outside of your city or state. You may also consider having check writing privileges but only on amounts above a certain amount like $250. This can help resist the urge to spend on little things help put a time buffer on when you think you want the money, and when you can actually get it.

One final note is to make sure your emergency fund is not in your 401(k), 403(b), traditional or Roth IRA. These are retirement accounts and should stay as such. A properly funded emergency fund will reduce if not eliminate any reliance on premature retirement account distributions.

Now, sit back, relax, and pray you don't need to use it!

THE ROTH IRA

Once you've established your emergency fund, it's time to continue to pay yourself first but for a sunny day in the future – your retirement. For most people (this includes you) the Roth IRA is going to be a great option to save money for retirement and have a tax-free source of income once they hit their golden years. The Roth IRA was named after its namesake, Senator William Roth of Delaware. The IRA part simply means Individual Retirement Arrangement.

Roth IRAs work like this: You save money into your Roth IRA on an after-tax basis. What this means is that when you get paid from your job and you've already paid Uncle Sam his share in taxes – you get what's left over. Of those leftovers (couldn't help the food reference) you can take some of that money and put it into a Roth IRA. This money then goes into an account of your choosing. This could be into mutual funds, stocks, bonds, ETFs, or even a simple savings account at your bank. There are a few things that are not allowed in IRAs such as life insurance and collectibles like art and antiques.

Over time your contributions, depending on how they're invested, will grow tax-deferred into a nice little nest egg ready for you to hatch at retirement. The magic of the Roth IRA really begins here. Remember when I said that after-tax money was going into the account? Well, since you've gone through the pain of having been taxed on that money already, any qualified withdrawals from your Roth IRA are now...wait for it...TAX FREE! Imagine an income source in retirement that cannot be taxed.

There are some great calculators online that can be used to show you how much you can have saved in 10, 20 or 30 years. I've included some websites you can visit at the end of the book.

As of 2026 you can contribute $7,500 annually to your Roth IRA and if you're age 50 or older, another $1,000 as a "catch-up" contribution. These numbers will generally increase periodically as inflation increases and as time goes on.

To see if a Roth IRA is an option for you to consider, talk with your financial professional and explore your options. Some good rules of thumb when looking at your options for funding a Roth IRA are to avoid mutual funds with high fees and expenses, insurance products (annuities) with high fees and surrender charges and complex products that are difficult for you (and your advisor) to understand and explain.

Finally, there are some income limitations for Roth IRA eligibility. If your Modified Adjusted Gross Income (MAGI) is too high (married filing jointly or single), you cannot *directly* contribute to a Roth IRA.

If you find yourself in this situation, consider the strategy called the "Backdoor" Roth IRA. This is where you open a traditional IRA, then *convert* that money to your Roth IRA.

For more information on IRAs, see IRS Publication 590.

YOUR EMPLOYER'S RETIREMENT PLAN

Whether you work as a doctor, teacher, office administrator, attorney, or government employee chances are you have access to your employer's retirement plan such as a 401(k), 403(b), 457, SEP, or SIMPLE. These plans are a great resource to save money into, and some employers will even *pay you* to participate!

Let's start with the 401(k). A 401(k) is a savings plan that is started by your employer to encourage both owners of the business and employees to save for retirement. Depending on how much you want to save, you can choose to have a specific dollar amount or percentage of your gross pay directed to your 401(k) account. Your money in your account can be invested tax-deferred in stock or bond mutual funds, company stock (if you work for a publicly traded company), or even a money market account.

Your choice of funds will depend on the company that offers the 401(k) through your employer. Generally, you're going to want to choose funds with low fees and expenses. As of 2026, the maximum amount you can put into your 401(k) is $24,500 annually and another $7,500 "catch-up" contribution if you're age 50 or older. At age 59 ½ qualified withdrawals are now taxed as ordinary income. Withdrawals before age 59 ½ are subject to penalties with some exceptions.

A cousin to the 401(k) is the 403(b). The 403(b) is very similar to the 401(k) in that you're allowed to allocate a certain amount or percentage of your gross pay to your account, tax-deferred. Where the 403(b) differs is that it's only allowed for non-profits such as school districts, hospitals, municipalities, and qualified charitable organizations. Another difference is by law the money in your 403(b) can only be invested in mutual funds or annuity contracts. You're not allowed to own individual stocks or bonds in it. Like the 401(k), you're allowed to save (as of 2026) $24,500 annually and another $7,500 "catch-up" contribution if you're age 50 or older. At age 59 ½ qualified withdrawals are now taxed as ordinary income. Withdrawals before age 59 ½ are subject to penalties with some exceptions.

Branching out in our retirement plan family tree we come to the 457 plan. 457 plans are reserved for certain non-profits such as hospitals, government entities, school districts and colleges and universities. As you may have guessed, 457 plans are like their 401(k) and 403(b) counterparts in that money from your gross pay goes into your account tax-deferred.

Like the 403(b) the 457 only allows investments in mutual funds or annuity contracts. Like the 401(k) and 403(b), you're allowed to save up to $24,500 annually and another $7,500 "catch-up" contribution if you're age 50 or older (for 2026).

Unlike the 401(k) and 403(b) the 457 allows you access to your money at any age, if you're separated from service from your employer. For example, if you were 40 years old and have been saving into a 457 since you were age 25 and you saved $50,000 and you were fired, laid off or resigned, you'd have access to your 457 money without penalty; you'd simply pay ordinary income tax on any withdrawals.

Another key point to make is regarding the aggregation rule. What this means is that you're only allowed to invest $24,500 (along with the "catch-up" if you qualify) *total* between a 401(k) and a 403(b). For example, you work as a professor for nine months of the year and save $14,000 in your college's 403(b). Over the summer, you work part time for a company that offers a 401(k) plan and you want to save money there. Assuming you're age 40, you'd only be able to save an additional $9,000 to your summer company's 401(k) – for a total of $24,500.

There is one exception to the aggregation rule. If you have access to a 401(k) or 403(b) and a 457, you can contribute the maximum to the 401(k) or 403(b) – for a total of $24,500 and then contribute the maximum to the 457 for an annual total of $49,000. The 457 trumps the aggregation rule. Few people may be able to sock away $49,000 (or $61,000 if over 50) per year, but it is available to those that work for employers offering both plans or if you work for two or more employers and they offer one or the other.

SEPs and SIMPLEs work a bit different. Typically, these plans are available to smaller employers and SEPs are common for those that are self-employed. Both SEPs and SIMPLEs use

IRAs as the funding vehicle to place retirement money, but each has different requirements as to contribution limits and participation requirements.

SEPs (Simplified Employee Pensions) can be funded to a maximum of $72,000 annually (for 2026) or 25% of the employee's salary – whichever is smaller. There can be corresponding tax deductions involved that may be beneficial for solo businesses or businesses with a small number of employees as there are requirements that *all* employees must participate.

SIMPLEs (Savings Incentive Match PLan for Employees) are another option for smaller businesses looking to start a retirement plan and looking for a cost-effective way to start (a 401(k) can be administratively expensive). Essentially, both employer and employees can participate, and certain rules dictate that the employer must make a matching contribution (hence the Match in the name) to participating employees. As of 2026, you can contribute a maximum of $17,000 annually to a SIMPLE plan with an additional "catch-up" contribution of $4,000 if you're age 50 or older.

Like SIMPLEs, some 401(k) and 403(b) plans also have the company match. This means that in addition to your contributions, your employer will also contribute or "match" to the amount you're contributing up to a certain percent. Consider taking full advantage of this. *It's free money!* There are several reasons why an employer would do this ranging from plan compliance to helping ensure employee satisfaction and loyalty.

Finally, participating in your employer's plan does not prohibit you from participating in a Traditional or Roth IRA. You can contribute the maximum allowed by law to both your employer's plan and your own IRA.

There are many nuances and details that are and aren't allowed between plans. Things can get pretty complicated the more access you have to retirement plans. It pays to do your due diligence, work with a professional and even *read* the IRS publications on retirement plans.

It goes without saying that before you decide to participate, talk with your human resources department (not your cubicle buddy) or a financial professional regarding your options and which option or combination is right for you.

PAY YOURSELF FIRST *(revisited)*

It's easy to save for retirement if you make it the first bill you pay. You can do this through fixed direct deposit, an employer retirement program or by getting on an automatic pay plan. It doesn't matter if it's only a small amount. What does matter is that you pay yourself first.

First, one of the easiest things you can do is take a portion of your paycheck and stick it right in the bank the day you get paid. If your employer allows direct deposit, take advantage of it.

Some employers even allow net and fixed direct deposit. Net direct deposit involves most of your paycheck going into your checking or savings account. Fixed direct deposit entails a small portion of the same paycheck going into a different account.

The beauty of this system is that you automatically put money into a separate savings account, and you never have to worry about remembering to save the money in the first place. After a few months, you may even forget about it until you receive your bank statement and see a nice sum already growing while you live comfortably on what's left.

If you get paid by paper check, you can set up a savings account with an automatic bill payment service. That way, when you cash your check and deposit it into your account, a certain sum is withdrawn from your checking account, into your savings account. This is the same as paying your bills automatically.

This way, you don't have to remember to consciously pay yourself. Treat your new savings account like a bill. Never miss a payment.

Another method: Have your bank automatically wire the money to your individual retirement account or participate in your employer's 401(k), 403(b), 457, SEP, SIMPLE or profit-sharing plan. The same concept applies where you dedicate a percentage or fixed amount from your paycheck every pay period. This saves money and lowers your taxes since these plans take money out on a pre-tax basis, meaning you're taxed on the sum left over after you've already saved.

I recommend starting out by saving 15% of your income. If that's a stretch for you, save 10% or even 5%. It's amazing how quickly it grows, and how easy it is to save even more.

Of course, money doesn't buy happiness, but can you remember how you felt the last time you found some stray cash on the street? Felt pretty good, didn't it? The same happens when you forget about what you're saving and find a tidy sum next time you open your statement.

WHY HIRE A PROFESSIONAL?

You can do plenty of things yourself, but for many tasks like managing your hard-earned savings, you need the skill and expertise of a professional. Especially when it comes to your finances, the professional's fees are paltry compared to the value they bring.

For mundane tasks we know we can do ourselves, it's second nature to roll up our sleeves and get the job done. For more complicated endeavors, there is no way you can go it alone.

You need to hire an attorney to make a will or help with a divorce. A real estate agent can walk you through the buying or selling of a home. You can increase your wealth by working with a financial advisor on your investments, financial plan or other money matters.

Some people say that some of these things can be done without the help of a pro. Granted there are plenty of do-it-yourself places for wills, trusts, investing and medical care. But let the buyer beware.

People who prefer going solo usually argue that it saves money. Sometimes, they have trust issues or they think they can do the job just as well if not better than the professional. Of course, a few DIY-ers get lucky, but many make unwise choices and don't realize the consequences until much later.

Take for example the person who does his own will online. Without an attorney or advisor to check it over, his heirs might belatedly find out that he made a mistake, or the will wasn't properly written, according to the state's laws.

In the business of financial planning, I see too many do-it-yourselfers play the stock market game by actively trading, watching cable news and reading money magazines. Do these amateurs really think they have an edge over thousands of Wall Street analysts and institutional investors? No wonder so many of them lose money and make terrible bets.

What should we as consumers look for when we hire help with financial matters? Here are some basics to look for:

- **Education**. Are they qualified and educated in their field? What degrees or designations do they hold?

- **Tenure**. How long have they practiced?

- **Licensing**. Are there state or federal standards needed for them to work in their profession?

- **What don't they know?** Are they willing to admit when they aren't qualified to help? Look at it this way: A medical general practitioner doesn't give you brain surgery. You need a brain surgeon. Both are doctors, but both have very different professions and clients. Likewise, an accountant can't help you make financial plans or allocate your investments properly.

- **Code of ethics**. Do they adhere to one?

- **Transparency**. Do you understand what they do for you, how they do it, and how they get paid?

This list is merely a good place to start. The main point is that you hire a professional for their expertise, experience and professional judgment.

You admit that you don't know everything, and you are ready to trust an expert to guide you.

In the long run, a professional potentially saves you money by avoiding mistakes and saving you time and energy that you can spend on more important tasks.

HOW FINANCIAL ADVISORS GET PAID

When you first meet with a financial advisor, it's important to ask not only how much his or her fees are, but *how you* pay. An advisor's compensation method can affect the type of advice you get, so you should understand the differences before you choose who to hire.

There are three ways financial advisors and planners are compensated: Commissions, fees, and a combination of both.

Here is what makes them different and relevant to you as an investor.

Commission. Some advisors get paid based on the products they sell. Commission rates vary between 5% and 50%, depending on the product. Term life insurance, for example, usually gives the advisor a commission of roughly 40% of the annual premium for the first year. Whole life insurance is generally 50% the first year. Term life policies, which cover you for a limited number of years, are generally less expensive than whole life, which continues if you pay the premiums and accumulates a cash value.

Other commissioned products include annuity products, individual stocks and bonds, and mutual funds purchased through a broker. Some mutual funds charge a load or commission on the initial purchase, or back-end load that charges you upon redeeming the investment.

Fee and Commission. Fee and commission is essentially a combination of commissions and fees. An advisor saying he or she is "fee-based" is an advisor that gets paid on commissions on certain products, and receives a fee on different products or services.

For example, an advisor who sells life insurance and annuities as well as investment management collects commissions for the life and annuity products and takes a flat fee or percentage of the assets in the investment management account.

Say you sign up for an asset management account where the annual fee is 2% to have your money professionally invested. You may only see a 2% charge for your fee, but the advisor who sold you the program may receive a commission. He should be forthcoming about this if you ask. This is generally seen in proprietary asset management programs of various companies and brokers. In both circumstances, the advisor is compensated by the product sold.

Fee-only. Fee-only advisors are paid for their advice, not on products they sell. Payment comes a few different ways. The first is strictly on an hourly basis or on retainer, like an attorney. They generally give you an estimate with a range of costs before giving you financial planning services.

Another way that advisors get paid is a flat fee for any assets of yours that they manage and invest for you. This can be as little as 0.25% or as high as 2%, depending on how much you invest. Some planners require a minimum level of assets to work with them and some do not. Most have a graduated fee schedule where your fee decreases as you invest more.

Many fee-only advisors offer to take you "off the clock" meaning that once you are billed by assets under management, they no longer charge you by the hour for advice and questions. Be careful of advisors that charge fees for both managing your money and hourly for planning. Make sure the advice is worth the extra money.

Fee-only is very transparent, meaning that you see exactly what you paying and what you paid for on your quarterly statement or invoice.

Lastly, always read the fine print and know exactly what you pay for. An advisor's compensation doesn't include the expense ratios and fees of the investments he puts you in. You might hire a fee-only advisor but if he puts you in a mutual fund that charges 1.5% in expenses don't be surprised when you see more than the advisor's 1% fee siphoned off. A commissioned advisor could sell you an annuity that has fund fees of 1.5% and policy charges of another 1.25%. This is another 2.75% of charges annually in addition to the commissions the advisor collects.

Your best approach is to be up-front: Ask about commissions and fees before you agree to buy a financial product. Have the advisor tell you how much he gets paid for convincing you to do something. If you don't like what you hear or don't understand the answer, think about soliciting another advisor's services. A good professional deserves to get paid, but his main goal should be to make more of your money work for you, not himself.

All three compensation types have their advantages and disadvantages. It all comes down to what sort of service you need and who you are comfortable with. Do your homework and ask lots of questions. Any advisor, no matter how they get paid, should put your best interests first and only make recommendations that are right for your personal situation.

Finally, look for an advisor who is a *fiduciary*. A fiduciary is legally obligated to act in your best interests. The best way to find out is to ask. If the answer is no, thank them for their time and find an advisor who is a fiduciary.

A NOTE ABOUT DESIGNATIONS

As you begin to seek advice regarding your savings and investments, you may come across professionals that have designations after their names – some might even have a can of alphabet soup! Here are some common designations you'll encounter when seeking out a professional. Your advisor should have a qualified designation as a *minimum requirement* before you start working with him or her.

CFP® - CERTIFIED FINANCIAL PLANNER™. This designation is considered the "gold standard" in the financial services industry. Holders of this designation are required to take college-level financial planning courses, have experience in financial planning, and must pass a rigorous 6-hour examination. The designation is owned and awarded by the CFP Board of Standards. www.cfp.net

ChFC® - Chartered Financial Consultant™. This designation is right in line with the CFP® with regards to the knowledge needed and required to earn the designation. Professionals that earn this mark must undertake 9 college courses in financial planning and endure 18 hours of total examination time. The designation is owned and awarded by The American College of Financial Services. www.chfchigheststandard.com

CPA - Certified Public Accountant. This designation is awarded to individuals that pass the rigorous Uniform Certified Public Accountant exam given by the American Institute of Certified Public Accountants. CPAs may be qualified to prepare tax returns and provide auditing services for companies. CPAs may also represent their clients in proceedings before the IRS. www.aicpa.org

CFA® - Chartered Financial Analyst™. This designation is pursued by individuals who have undertaken studies in security analysis, stocks, bonds, investment management and corporate finance. Individuals must endure three levels of examinations before the designation is awarded. Many mutual fund managers, pension fund managers and endowment managers have this credential. www.cfainstitute.org

EA - Enrolled Agent. The enrolled agent designation is awarded to individuals who pass three different IRS exams involving personal taxation, business taxation and general tax principles. Like CPAs, enrolled agents may also represent their clients in in tax proceedings before the IRS. www.irs.gov/Tax-Professionals/Enrolled-Agents

CLOSING THOUGHTS

By now you've reached the end of this book and have hopefully began to think about what your next steps will be or perhaps have already gotten started on some of the ideas presented earlier.

My best advice is to start today – and start with my favorite food – *cold turkey*. Do I really mean refrigerated cold cuts of poultry? Not really. What I do mean is getting started as soon as you can, with as much as you can right away and discarding bad habits *today*.

Sometimes people make the mistake of saying "I'll start next week as soon as this week is done." Or they might be thinking, "I'll start exercising next week and just focus on my eating now."

Procrastination works – *against you*.

One of your best bets is going to be to start making as many positive lifestyle and habit changes as you can. The momentum will carry you further than you can imagine and give you more incentive to stay on track than if you just "try it" or engage half-heartedly.

According to a study done by Stanford University, making changes to both eating habits and exercise habits at the same time made it more likely for people to maintain those changes for longer periods of time, versus trying to change eating habits first, then focusing on exercise and vice versa.

Regarding starting to save, log on to your bank account now and allocate a dollar amount or percent to your savings and emergency fund. When you get to work ask your HR department if they have a 401(k) or another savings plan and how can you get started saving. Ask if they have a direct deposit form for your paycheck if you're not already doing so. Need advice? Call and set up appointments to meet with and interview a few financial advisors.

Start writing down your goals for the next week, the next month, and for the next year. Keep track of your progress. You'll be amazed at what you did when you revisit and revise your goals next year at this time.

And finally, have fun! Make it interesting for yourself. Find activities and exercises that you love to do and enjoy. Reward yourself. When you hit a goal, do something special and fun. Get your family involved. If you have kids, they can learn some excellent eating, exercise, and money habits at a young age — and they'll be forever grateful. Talk about a great investment!

And please let me know how you're doing. I welcome your comments, thoughts, questions, and progress reports. Drop me a note at sterling.raskie@gmail.com and share your results.

Best of luck and success to you!

www.ingramcontent.com/pod-product-compliance
Lightning Source LLC
Chambersburg PA
CBHW071716170526
45165CB00005B/2038